SPELLING 3

FOR YOUNG CATHOLICS

Written by
Seton Staff

Seton Press
Front Royal, VA

J.M.J.

Executive Editor: Dr. Mary Kay Clark
Editors: Seton Staff

© 2013 Seton Home Study School
All rights reserved.
Printed in the United States of America

Seton Home Study School
1350 Progress Drive
Front Royal, VA 22630
Phone: (540) 636-9990
Fax: (540) 636-1602

For more information, visit us on the Web at: www.setonhome.org
Contact us by e-mail at: info@setonhome.org

ISBN: 978-1-60704-062-0

Cover: *The Madonna and Child with St. Elizabeth and the Infant St. John* by Peter Paul Rubens

J.M.J.

Dedicated to the Sacred Heart of Jesus

J.M.J.

Jesus, Mary, and Joseph, pray for us.

J.M.J.

Spelling 3 for Young Catholics

CONTENTS

Introduction:	Notes for Parents	vii
Lesson 1:	Sight words	2
Lesson 2:	Compound words	8
Lesson 3:	/aa/ sound in **at**	12
Lesson 4:	/eh/ sound in **egg**	18
Lesson 5:	/ih/ sound in **it**	22
Lesson 6:	/ah/ sound in **ox**	28
Lesson 7:	/aw/ sound in **awe**	32
Lesson 8:	/uh/ sound in **us**	38
Lesson 9:	First Quarter Review	42
Lesson 10:	/k/ sound in **c**at, /s/ sound in **s**at	44
Lesson 11:	/j/ sound in **j**am, /z/ sound in **z**oo	50
Lesson 12:	Silent consonants	54
Lesson 13:	/ng/ sound in si**ng**	60
Lesson 14:	/ay/ sound in **a**te	64
Lesson 15:	/ee/ sound in **e**ve	70
Lesson 16:	/iy/ sound in **i**ce	74
Lesson 17:	/oh/ sound in **o**ak	80
Lesson 18:	Second Quarter Review	84
Lesson 19:	/yoo/ sound in **u**se	86
Lesson 20:	/ooh/ sound in **oo**ze	92
Lesson 21:	/uu/ sound in b**oo**k	96
Lesson 22:	/uhr/ sound in **ur**n	102
Lesson 23:	/ahr/ sound in **ar**k	106
Lesson 24:	/ayr/ sound in **air**	112
Lesson 25:	/eer/ sound in **ear**	116
Lesson 26:	/ohr/ sound in **oar**	122
Lesson 27:	Third Quarter Review	126
Lesson 28:	/ou/ sound in **ou**t	128
Lesson 29:	/oi/ sound in **oi**l	134
Lesson 30:	/sh/ sound in **sh**eep	138
Lesson 31:	Ending -**le** sound in Bib**le**	144
Lesson 32:	Plurals -**s**, -**es**	148
Lesson 33:	Ending -**ing**	154
Lesson 34:	Ending -**ed**	158
Lesson 35:	Suffixes -**ly**, -**ful**	164
Lesson 36	Fourth Quarter Review	168
Alphabetized Word List		170
Spelling Vowel Sounds		172
Spelling Consonant Sounds		173
Spelling Rules		174
Answer Key		178
List of Artists		191

Jesus, Mary, Joseph, I love You. Save souls!

J.M.J.

Jesus was obedient to Mary and Joseph.

J.M.J.

Notes for Parents

Preface

We are pleased to present this Catholic speller for your children. In light of the Vatican's directive for schools to incorporate the Catholic Faith throughout the curriculum, we have made an effort to include Catholic themes and culture in the text. We hope that your child enjoys learning to spell with this Catholic speller.

Introduction

Spelling 3 for Young Catholics presents a quick review of previously taught lessons, as well as a presentation of new lessons. The focus in *Spelling 1 for Young Catholics* and *Spelling 2 for Young Catholics* was to teach your child how to spell by listening to letter sounds and identifying regular spelling patterns. The focus in *Spelling 3 for Young Catholics* extends beyond learning how to spell words with regular spelling patterns to becoming proficient in memorizing and spelling frequently occurring words with irregular spellings. Through the lessons in this book, your child will learn to spell words containing regular and irregular spelling patterns. The memorization of frequently occurring words containing irregular spellings will enable your child to apply newly acquired spelling skills to daily writing assignments.

Pretest

After completing two years of spelling lessons, children usually are proficient in spelling short and long vowel words containing consonant blends. Your child should be able to spell words with regular spellings of short and long vowel sounds simply by listening to the sounds of the letters. Even if your child knows how to spell some of these words, completing the exercises will help your child to learn the spelling patterns and rules that apply to other words.

Spelling Versus Phonics

There is a major difference between spelling and phonics. **Spelling** emphasizes *different spellings of the same sounds*, such as the sound /uu/ in the words b**oo**k and b**u**sh. **Phonics** distinguishes between *different sounds in words that are similarly spelled*. For example, a spelling lesson on words containing the sound of /uu/ as in b**oo**k would include words of different spellings of this sound, such as b**oo**k and b**u**sh. A phonics lesson would take words like b**oo**k /uu/ and b**oo**t /oo/ with the same spelling of the letters **oo**, and then sort them by the phonetic sounds in these words—that is, /uu/ and /oo/ in this case. The letters **oo** are the same in each spelling word but are pronounced differently.

Jesus, Mary, Joseph, I love You. Save souls!

J.M.J.

This book teaches the most common spellings for each sound. Words that do not follow a spelling pattern are called *sight words*. These words have unique spellings, which must be memorized.

Accented Vowel Sounds: Short, Long, Other

Phonics concepts are taught in isolated units, whereas spelling lessons must be grouped (after the separate phonics lessons have been taught) so that the student can distinguish the different spellings of the same sounds. The phonics concepts in *Spelling 3 for Young Catholics* have been taught as separate lessons in our phonics books. We have grouped the majority of the spelling words in *Spelling 3 for Young Catholics* by the vowel sounds: the short vowel sounds, the long vowel sounds, and the other vowel sounds.

Pronunciation symbols for vowel and consonant sounds vary among different dictionaries. In this book, letter combinations are used as pronunciation symbols. If you wish, you may show your child the pronunciation symbols used in your dictionary at home. It is not necessary, however, for your child to memorize a specific set of pronunciation symbols. What is important is that your child identify the sounds and memorize the spellings that represent each sound. Identifying the sounds is an auditory exercise, whereas memorizing the spellings is a visual exercise.

Note the following pronunciation symbols for the vowel sounds:

Short Vowel Sounds	Long Vowel Sounds	Other Vowel Sounds
the /aa/ sound in **at**	the /ay/ sound in **at**e	the /aw/ sound in **aw**e
the /eh/ sound in **e**gg	the /ee/ sound in **e**ve	the /ooh/ sound in **oo**ze
the /ih/ sound in **it**	the /iy/ sound in **i**ce	the /uu/ sound in b**oo**k
the /ah/ sound in **ox**	the /oh/ sound in **o**ak	the /ou/ sound in **ou**t
the /uh/ sound in **us**	the /yoo/ sound in **u**se	the /oi/ sound in **oi**l

Some dictionaries use different pronunciation symbols for vowels followed by the consonant **r** because the pronunciation of some **r**-controlled words varies among different dialects. In this book, the pronunciation symbol for the vowel sound is combined with the symbol for the sound of **r**. Note this combination in the following symbols for **r**-controlled vowel sounds: the /ahr/ sound in **ar**k, the /uhr/ sound in **ur**n, the /ayr/ sound in **air**, the /eer/ sound in **ear**, and the /ohr/ sound in **oar**.

Using This Book

There are thirty-six lessons in this book, one for each week of the academic year. The last lesson of each quarter is a quarterly review in preparation for the quarterly test. Except for the quarterly reviews, each lesson includes four pages, one for each of the first four days in the school week. On the fifth day of each week, please administer a spelling test.

In the back of this book is an alphabetical list of the spelling words, followed by a list of spelling rules and an Answer Key. If you wish, you may tear the Answer Key out of the back of the book for your use.

Jesus, Mary, Joseph, I love You. Save souls!

J.M.J.

Bonus Word

Each word list includes one bonus word. The bonus word may be more difficult than the other words in the list. Although bonus words are not included on quarter tests, your child should study the bonus word along with the other words in each word list. When grading the weekly tests, divide the total number of correct words by 15 rather than 16 total words. In this way, the bonus word can provide your child with bonus points in the weekly test grade. For example, if your child spells all words correctly, including the bonus word, divide 16 by 15 to calculate a score of 107%. On the other hand, if your child misspells one word, either the bonus word or another word, divide 15 by 15 to calculate a score of 100%. With this grading strategy, your child will quickly learn the advantage of paying careful attention to the bonus word.

Instructions for Daily Exercises

Day 1: This is the most important lesson for the week. Read the spelling rule at the top of the page. The letters between the slashes, such as **/ay/**, are pronounced by the sound of the spelling in the sample word. Say the sound of the spelling rather than reciting the letters. Note the application of the rule in each spelling word. Pronounce each spelling word for correct spelling. Spell each word aloud, then repeat the word. Complete the exercise using words from the spelling list. Start with the first word in the list. Find the spelling of the sound in the exercise that matches the spelling of the sound in the word. Write the word in the section that corresponds to the spelling. Check your spelling. It is very important to spell the word correctly in this lesson. Continue this exercise with each additional word on the list.

Day 2: Fill in the blanks of the sentences using the spelling words from the lesson. Start with the first sentence. Find the list word that fits in the blank. Write this word in the blank, then cross it off the list. Each list word may be used only once in this exercise. Try to spell each word without looking at the word list. Check your spelling. If you misspelled the word, erase it and write it correctly. Continue this exercise with each additional sentence. Say the word; read the complete sentence; then repeat the word.

Day 3: Write the spelling words in alphabetical order on the left side of the page. Read and discuss the spelling tips, which are important concepts leading into further lessons. Complete the exercises using spelling words from the lesson. These exercises include writing list words that are homophones, rhyming words, and/or words having the indicated syllables. Check your spelling. Correct any misspelled words and rewrite them five times each. Some of these exercises have more than one possible answer. Only one answer is required. The Answer Key includes all possible answers. Remember that homophones are words that have the same pronunciation but different spellings and meanings. Memorizing the spelling of homophones will help you to remember the spelling patterns for other words.

Jesus, Mary, Joseph, I love You. Save souls!

Day 4: Take the pretest. Spell aloud and trace the spelling words. Fold the paper in half, turning the words under so that they cannot be seen. Listen to the words as they are dictated alone and within a sentence. Write each word carefully. Unfold the paper and check your spelling immediately after completing the pretest. Correct any misspelled words, and rewrite them five times each.

Day 5: Take the spelling test for this week. Listen to the words as they are dictated alone and within a sentence. Write each word carefully on a separate sheet of paper. Correct any misspelled words, and rewrite them five times each.

Becoming a Proficient Speller

Experts tell us that in order to learn to spell most effectively, it is best to combine the use of three of our senses. We use our auditory sense (hearing) when we pronounce the word or hear it pronounced. We use the visual sense (seeing) when we look at the word and make a mental image of it (memory). We use the kinesthetic sense (touch) when we physically write the word. Since identifying the sounds in words phonetically is an auditory (hearing) exercise, whereas memorizing the spelling of words is a visual (seeing) exercise, we can use visual aids, such as flash cards, in learning how to spell. Here are the steps to follow:

1. Write the spelling words on flash cards.

2. Take a mental snapshot of each word. Blink your eyes like the shutter of a camera, and hold them closed for a few seconds.

3. Spell the word out loud as you commit it to memory.

J.M.J.

Ask Our Blessed Mother to pray for you to be a good speller.

LESSON 1

Sight words

gone
sew
once
eye
else
is
only
been
from
one
quiet
shall
two
as
shoe

BONUS

laugh

Week One: Day 1

Sight words have irregular spellings.

A Sort by Syllable
Say each list word out loud. If the word has one syllable, write it in the first box below. If the word has two syllables, write it in the second box below.

1 syllable

gone
sew
once
eye
else
is
been
from
one
shall
two
as
shoe
laugh

2 syllables

only
quiet

Jesus, Mary, Joseph, I love You. Save souls!

J.M.J.

B Complete the Sentence

Starting with the first sentence, find the list word that completes the sentence. Write the word in the blank. Use each word only once.

1. I love my sisters as much __as__ I love my brothers.

2. My mother __is__ the best teacher for me.

3. There is only __one__ God.

4. Only __once__ did Mother tell me to do my chores.

5. Last year, I received __two__ sacraments.

6. I helped my little brother find his missing __shoe__.

7. Dad drove __from__ work to home in a half hour.

8. By 8:00 p.m., all the children had __gone__ to bed.

9. Jesus said that the pure of heart __shall__ see God.

10. I can __sew__ a button on my shirt.

11. The doctor put a patch on Daniel's left __eye__.

12. I have __been__ studying my spelling words.

13. We brought something __else__ for the poor children.

14. My cousin has five sisters and __only__ one brother.

15. When the baby is sleeping, I am __quiet__.

16. Saint Philip Neri liked to __laugh__.

Jesus, Mary, Joseph, I love You. Save souls!

Week One: Day 3 J.M.J.

C Alphabetical Order

1. as
2. been
3. else
4. eye
5. from
6. gone
7. is
8. ~~~~ laugh
9. once
10. one
11. only
12. quiet
13. ~~~~ sew
14. ~~shoe~~ shall
15. ~~~~ shoe
16. two

Tips from your *Guardian Angel*

- Sight words must be memorized because they do not follow regular spelling rules.
- A one-syllable word cannot be divided.
- Each syllable has only one vowel sound.
- The letters **q** and **u** always go together to make the **/kw/** sound, as in **qu**it.
- Divide between two vowels when they each make their own sound, as in qu**i**·**e**t.
- The **/f/** sound in **f**an is spelled **f** (**f**an), **ff** (stu**ff**), **ph** (**ph**one), or **gh** (lau**gh**).
- A homophone is a word that sounds the same as another word but has a different spelling and meaning.

D Write the Homophones

1. bin

   been

2. too

   two

3. I

   is

4. won

   one

5. so

   sew

J.M.J.

St. Philip Neri liked to laugh.

Pretest

J.M.J. Week One: Day 4

Fold this page on the dotted line.
As you hear each dictated word, write it on the line.
When you are done, unfold the page and check your work.

1. gone	1. gone
2. sew	2. sew
3. once	3. once
4. eye	4. eye
5. else	5. else
6. is	6. is
7. only	7. only
8. been	8. been
9. from	9. from
10. one	10. one
11. quiet	11. quiet
12. shall	12. shall
13. two	13. two
14. as	14. as
15. shoe	15. shoe
16. laugh	16. laugh

Jesus, Mary, Joseph, I love You. Save souls!

5

J.M.J.

St. Luke used a paintbrush to paint the Blessed Mother and Baby Jesus.

LESSON 2

Compound words

Week Two: Day 1

Compound words are made up of smaller words. Divide a compound word between these smaller words.

A Identify the Words with These Syllables

Divide each list word into two smaller words. Write the first word on the left side of the dotted line, and the second word on the right side of the dotted line. Each smaller word is a syllable of the compound word.

- pancake
- grapevine
- cannot
- homework
- raindrop
- paintbrush
- grownup
- sidewalk
- backpack
- farmland
- sailboat
- bathtub
- farmyard
- cowboy
- playground

BONUS
- mousetrap

pan	cake
grape	vine
can	not
home	work
rain	drop
paint	brush
grown	up
side	walk
back	pack
farm	land
sail	boat
bath	tub
farm	yard
cow	boy
play	ground
mouse	trap

J.M.J. Week Two: Day 2

B Complete the Sentence

Starting with the first sentence, find the list word that completes the sentence. Write the word in the blank. Use each word only once.

1. I helped Mom clean the __bathtub__ after my bath.

2. I __cannot__ learn how to spell unless I study.

3. A __sailboat__ needs wind to move on the water.

4. Timmy said grace before he ate the __pancake__.

5. A __cowboy__ rides a horse on a ranch.

6. Mom takes us to the __playground__ on sunny days.

7. I am a child, and Dad is a __grownup__.

8. I do my __homework__ while Mom teaches my sisters.

9. Grapes grow on a __grapevine__.

10. It is safer to walk on a __sidewalk__ than on a street.

11. Carry your belongings in your __backpack__.

12. Food crops are grown on __farmland__.

13. A __farmyard__ is next to farm buildings.

14. When I felt a __raindrop__, I put up my umbrella.

15. In art class, I used a __paintbrush__ to paint a cross.

16. Dad found a mouse in the __mousetrap__.

Jesus, Mary, Joseph, I love You. Save souls!

Week Two: Day 3 J.M.J.

C Alphabetical Order

1. backpack
2. bathtub
3. cannot
4. cowboy
5. farmland
6. farmyard
7. grapevine
8. grownup
9. homework
10. mousetrap
11. pantbrush
12. pancake
13. playground
14. raindrop
15. sailboat
16. sidewalk

Tips from your *Guardian Angel*

- In compound words, each syllable is a smaller word.
- To determine whether a syllable is stressed or unstressed, clap the syllables as you say the word. The stressed syllables should have a louder clap.

D Write the Homophones from the Smaller Words within the List Words

1. groan

    grown

2. sale

    sail

E Write the Rhyming Words from the Smaller Words within the List Words

1. house

    mouse

2. hand

    land

3. hard

    yard

4. toy

    boy

5. found

    ground

6. math

    bath

Jesus, Mary, Joseph, I love You. Save souls!

Pretest

J.M.J.   Week Two: Day 4

> Fold this page on the dotted line.
> As you hear each dictated word, write it on the line.
> When you are done, unfold the page and check your work.

1. pancake
2. grapevine
3. cannot
4. homework
5. raindrop
6. paintbrush
7. grownup
8. sidewalk
9. backpack
10. farmland
11. sailboat
12. bathtub
13. farmyard
14. cowboy
15. playground
16. mousetrap

1. pancake
2. grapevine
3. cannot
4. homework
5. raindrop
6. paintbrush
7. grownup
8. sidewalk
9. backpack
10. farmland
11. sailboat
12. bathtub
13. farmyard
14. cowboy
15. playground
16. mousetrap

Jesus, Mary, Joseph, I love You. Save souls!

LESSON 3

/aa/ sound in at

The **/aa/** sound in **a**t is usually spelled **a**.

cavity
contact
subtract
after
rabbit
napkin
answer
sandwich
Advent
began
catfish
admit
animal
branch
baptize

BONUS

Catholic

J.M.J.   Week Three: Day 1

A Sort by Syllable
Each syllable has its own vowel sound. Identify the syllable in each word that has the **/aa/** sound in **a**t. Sort the words by the number of syllables. (Parent: Review the "Notes to Parents" in the introductory pages.)

1 syllable	branch
	admit
	contact
	subtract
	rabbit
	napkin
	answer
2 syllables	sandwich
	catfish
	after
	baptize
	Advent
	began
	animal
3 syllables	cavity
	Catholic

J.M.J.   Week Three: Day 2

B Complete the Sentence

Starting with the first sentence, find the list word that completes the sentence. Write the word in the blank. Use each word only once.

1. A _brach_ grows out from the trunk of a tree.

2. I can add and _subtract_ numbers in my math book.

3. We must do our penance _after_ we go to Confession.

4. My pet _rabbit_ ate the lettuce in our garden.

5. Mary made a tuna _sandwich_ for her little sister.

6. Peter lit the pink candle on the _Advent_ wreath.

7. I place a _napkin_ on my lap while I eat.

8. Please _answer_ the telephone, Anne.

9. When I confess my sins, I _admit_ my guilt.

10. I wanted to _contact_ my friend, so I wrote a letter.

11. Mass _began_ at 8:00 a.m. yesterday.

12. A _catfish_ looks like it has cat whiskers.

13. Father Joseph will _Baptize_ my baby sister on Sunday.

14. Brush your teeth, Lucy, so that you don't get a _cavity_.

15. The largest _animal_ on Earth is the blue whale.

16. Jesus started the _Catholic_ Church.

Jesus, Mary, Joseph, I love You. Save souls!

Week Three: Day 3 	 J.M.J.

C Alphabetical Order

1. ad-mit
2. ~~scribble~~ Advent
3. after
4. animal
5. answer
6. baptize
7. began
8. branch
9. catfish
10. catholic
11. cavity
12. contact
13. napkin
14. rabbit
15. sandwich
16. subtract

Tips from your *Guardian Angel*

- A proper noun begins with a capital letter.
- Dividing big words into small syllables can help you to learn the correct spelling.
- Divide between two consonants, as in af·ter. However, do not divide between two consonants that make one sound (a digraph), as in the word tel·e·**ph**one.
- Divide before and after a vowel that makes its own sound, as in cav·**i**·ty.
- Use the strategy of pronouncing for correct spelling to remember double consonants in a multi-syllable word, such as ra**b**·**b**it. Pronouncing the consonant twice will help you remember to write it twice.

D Write the Words with These Syllables

1. sub
   sub-tract
2. nap
   nap-kin
3. sand
   Sand-wich
4. vent
   Ad-vent
5. an
   beg-an

Jesus, Mary, Joseph, I love You. Save souls!

J.M.J.   Week Three: Day 4

Pretest

Fold this page on the dotted line.
As you hear each dictated word, write it on the line.
When you are done, unfold the page and check your work.

1. cavity
2. contact
3. subtract
4. after
5. rabbit
6. napkin
7. answer
8. sandwich
9. Advent
10. began
11. catfish
12. admit
13. animal
14. branch
15. baptize
16. Catholic

1. cavity
2. contact
3. subtract
4. after
5. rabbit
6. napkin
7. answer
8. sandwich
9. Advent
10. began
11. catfish
12. admit
13. animal
14. branch
15. baptize
16. Catholic

Jesus, Mary, Joseph, I love You. Save souls!

J.M.J.

Jesus came and asked St. John to baptize him in the Jordan River.

J.M.J.

The Parable of the Prodigal Son teaches a lesson about God's love.

LESSON 4

J.M.J.   Week Four: Day 1

> The /eh/ sound in **e**gg is usually spelled **e** or **ea**.
> Sight words have unusual spellings.

/eh/ sound in **e**gg

letter
bread
again
read
confess
any
head
many
spread
dead
second
Heaven
lesson
breakfast
never

BONUS

telephone

A. Sort by Spelling

Each box below has a different spelling of the **/eh/** sound in **e**gg. On each line, write a list word that has the same spelling of this sound as the one in the box.

e	letter
	confess
	second
	lesson
	never
	telephone
ea	bread
	read
	head
	spread
	dead
	Heaven
	breakfast
Sight words	again
	any
	many

Jesus, Mary, Joseph, I love You. Save souls!

J.M.J. Week Four: Day 2

B Complete the Sentence
Starting with the first sentence, find the list word that completes the sentence. Write the word in the blank. Use each word only once.

1. We put the __bread__ in the toaster.

2. Eating a good __breakfast__ helps me to feel well.

3. God wants me to be happy with Him in __Heaven__.

4. Write a __letter__ to Grandmother.

5. Jesus used parables to teach a __lesson__.

6. Saint Dominic Savio vowed __never__ to sin.

7. Have you __read__ the Bible today?

8. When I __confess__ my sins, Jesus forgives me.

9. The cat carried a __dead__ mouse in its mouth.

10. God knows the number of hairs on my __head__.

11. One __second__ is a very short period of time.

12. Our Blessed Mother never committed __any__ sins.

13. John has __many__ colored pencils.

14. Study the spelling words __again__.

15. The people __spread__ palms on the ground for Jesus.

16. Answer the __telephone__ politely.

Jesus, Mary, Joseph, I love You. Save souls!

Week Four: Day 3   J.M.J.

C Alphabetical Order

1. agian
2. any
3. bread
4. breakfast
5. confess
6. dead
7. head
8. Heaven
9. lesson
10. letter
11. many
12. never
13. read
14. second
15. spread
16. Telephone

Tip from your *Guardian Angel*

> Divide after the consonant when a short vowel sound is followed by a consonant and another vowel, as in H**eav**·en.

D Write the Homophones

1. red

    read

2. lessen

    lesson

E Write the Rhyming Words

1. clever

    never

2. seven

    Heaven

3. amen

    again

F Write the Words with These Syllables

1. fast

    break-fast

2. phone

    tele-phone

3. let

    let-ter

Jesus, Mary, Joseph, I love You. Save souls!

Pretest

J.M.J.

Week Four: Day 4

Fold this page on the dotted line.
As you hear each dictated word, write it on the line.
When you are done, unfold the page and check your work.

1. letter
2. bread
3. agian *again*
4. read
5. confess
6. any
7. head
8. many
9. spread
10. dead
11. second
12. Heaven
13. lesson
14. breakfast
15. never
16. telephone

1. letter
2. bread
3. again
4. read
5. confess
6. any
7. head
8. many
9. spread
10. dead
11. second
12. Heaven
13. lesson
14. breakfast
15. never
16. telephone

Jesus, Mary, Joseph, I love You. Save souls!

LESSON 5

/ih/ sound in it

give
picture
pitcher
minute
hidden
hymnal
different
myth
Indian
build
river
gypsy
begin
children
live

BONUS

America

again

J.M.J.   Week Five: Day 1

The **/ih/** sound in **it** is usually spelled **i**, **y**, or **ui**.

A Sort by Spelling

Each box below has a different spelling of the **/ih/** sound in **it**. On each line, write a list word that has the same spelling as the one in the box.

i	_____ _____ _____ _____ _____ _____ _____ _____ _____ _____ _____
y	_____ _____ _____
ui	_____

Jesus, Mary, Joseph, I love You. Save souls!

B Complete the Sentence

Starting with the first sentence, find the list word that completes the sentence. Write the word in the blank. Use each word only once.

1. A Bible story is true; it is not a _____.

2. The caterpillar changed into a _____ moth.

3. We sing hymns from the _____.

4. Dad will _____ a tree house for us.

5. A _____ of our family hangs on the wall.

6. Pour the lemonade from the yellow _____.

7. There are sixty seconds in one _____.

8. _____ each day with a prayer.

9. Jesus said, "Let the little _____ come to Me."

10. Joseph has _____ behind the curtain.

11. God made rainbows with many _____ colors.

12. Blessed Kateri Tekakwitha was an _____.

13. The _____ flows into the ocean.

14. Thomas will _____ his drawings to his mother.

15. We _____ in a brick house.

16. _____ is a free country.

Week Five: Day 3 J.M.J.

C Alphabetical Order

1.
2.
3.
4.
5.
6.
7.
8.
9.
10.
11.
12.
13.
14.
15.
16.

Tips from your *Guardian Angel*

- The **/v/** sound at the end of a word is never spelled **v**. It is usually spelled **ve**, as in gi**ve** and li**ve**. Usually, only long vowel words have a final silent **e**, as in li**fe**.
- The words picture and pitcher sound similar, but they are not homophones. The **c** in pi**c**·ture makes the **/k/** sound in c**a**t, but the **tch** in pi**tch**·er makes the **/ch/** sound in **ch**ur**ch**.

D Write the Rhyming Words

1. with

2. filled

3. liver

4. give

E Write the Words with These Syllables

1. hid

2. in

3. gin

24 *Jesus, Mary, Joseph, I love You. Save souls!*

Pretest

J.M.J. Week Five: Day 4

Fold this page on the dotted line.
As you hear each dictated word, write it on the line.
When you are done, unfold the page and check your work.

1.	1. give
2.	2. picture
3.	3. pitcher
4.	4. minute
5.	5. hidden
6.	6. hymnal
7.	7. different
8.	8. myth
9.	9. Indian
10.	10. build
11.	11. river
12.	12. gypsy
13.	13. begin
14.	14. children
15.	15. live
16.	16. America

Jesus, Mary, Joseph, I love You. Save souls!

J.M.J.

Jesus said, "Let the little children come to Me."

J.M.J.

St. Peter was an Apostle of the Lord Jesus Christ.

LESSON 6

/ah/ sound in ox

father
upon
watch
Amen
wand
beyond
homily
dollar
hurrah
honor
lot
wander
koala
boxes
doctor

BONUS

apostle

J.M.J. Week Six: Day 1

The **/ah/** sound in **o**x is spelled **o** or **a**.

A Sort by Spelling
Each box below has a different spelling of the same sound. On each line, write a list word that has the same spelling as the one in the box.

o

_____

_____

_____

_____

_____

_____

_____

a

_____

_____

_____

_____

_____

_____

_____

_____

Jesus, Mary, Joseph, I love You. Save souls!

Week Six: Day 2

B Complete the Sentence

Starting with the first sentence, find the list word that completes the sentence. Write the word in the blank. Use each word only once.

1. Many _____ were packed in the truck.

2. The garden is _____ the fence.

3. Everyone listened to the pastor's _____.

4. There are one hundred cents in one _____.

5. Saint Joan sat _____ a rock near the stream.

6. At the end of a prayer, we say, "_____."

7. _____! We won the game!

8. _____ reads a Bible story to us at bedtime.

9. The _____ lives in a tree.

10. _____ your father and your mother.

11. The _____ gave medicine to my sick brother.

12. Grandpa built his house on the empty _____.

13. The conductor's _____ looked like a stick.

14. Don't _____ alone in the park.

15. _____ the ball carefully.

16. Saint Peter was an _____ of the Lord Jesus Christ.

Jesus, Mary, Joseph, I love You. Save souls!

Week Six: Day 3   J.M.J.

C Alphabetical Order

1.
2.
3.
4.
5.
6.
7.
8.
9.
10.
11.
12.
13.
14.
15.
16.

> **Tips** from your *Guardian Angel*
>
> 🕊 The **/ch/** sound in **ch**ew can be spelled **tch** (wa**tch**).
> 🕊 The word **Amen** is an interjection that means "so be it."
> 🕊 Interjections are usually capitalized.

D Write the Rhyming Words

1. notch

2. pond

3. collar

4. pot

5. foxes

6. fossil

E Write the Words with These Syllables

1. men

2. up

Jesus, Mary, Joseph, I love You. Save souls!

J.M.J. Week Six: Day 4

Pretest

Fold this page on the dotted line.
As you hear each dictated word, write it on the line.
When you are done, unfold the page and check your work.

1. father
2. upon
3. watch
4. Amen
5. wand
6. beyond
7. homily
8. dollar
9. hurrah
10. honor
11. lot
12. wander
13. koala
14. boxes
15. doctor
16. apostle

Jesus, Mary, Joseph, I love You. Save souls!

LESSON 7

/aw/ sound in awe

saw
thought
often
yawn
taught
always
soggy
pause
awful
awe
sauce
water
also
because
mall

BONUS

daughter

Week Seven: Day 1

The **/aw/** sound in **awe** is usually spelled **a**, **o**, **aw**, **au**, or **ough**. Sometimes it is spelled **augh**.

A Sort by Spelling

Each box below has a different spelling of the **/aw/** sound in **awe**. On each line, write a list word that has the same spelling of this sound as the one in the box.

a	
o	
aw	
au	
ough	
augh	

J.M.J.   Week Seven: Day 2

B Complete the Sentence
Starting with the first sentence, find the list word that completes the sentence. Write the word in the blank. Use each word only once.

1. The shepherds looked at Jesus with _____.

2. The Three Kings _____ Baby Jesus.

3. The sour milk tasted _____.

4. Pray the Rosary as _____ as you can.

5. Tired children _____ before bedtime.

6. Jesus said, "I am with you _____."

7. The _____ shoes dried near the fireplace.

8. My baby sister cried _____ she was hungry.

9. _____ before walking across the street.

10. Spoon the _____ on the meat carefully.

11. Drink plenty of _____ every day.

12. Some families go to the _____ to buy shoes.

13. Jesus is God, but He is _____ a man.

14. My mother _____ me how to pray.

15. I _____ I knew how to spell these words.

16. Mr. Jones is proud of his _____.

Jesus, Mary, Joseph, I love You. Save souls!

Week Seven: Day 3   J.M.J.

C Alphabetical Order

1. _____
2. _____
3. _____
4. _____
5. _____
6. _____
7. _____
8. _____
9. _____
10. _____
11. _____
12. _____
13. _____
14. _____
15. _____
16. _____

> **Tips** from your *Guardian Angel*
>
> - **All** is usually spelled with one **l** when another syllable is added to it, as in al·ways and al·so.
> - Usually, double the final **l, f,** or **s** after a single vowel in a one-syllable word (ma**ll**, stu**ff**, Ma**ss**).
> - The spelling **au** is usually used within a root (p**au**se). The spelling **aw** is often used at the end of a root (p**aw**).

D Write the Homophones

1. taut _____
2. paws _____
3. maul _____

E Write the Rhyming Words

1. foggy _____
2. fought _____
3. lawn _____
4. hall _____

Pretest

J.M.J.

Week Seven: Day 4

Fold this page on the dotted line.
As you hear each dictated word, write it on the line.
When you are done, unfold the page and check your work.

1.
2.
3.
4.
5.
6.
7.
8.
9.
10.
11.
12.
13.
14.
15.
16.

1. saw
2. thought
3. often
4. yawn
5. taught
6. always
7. soggy
8. pause
9. awful
10. awe
11. sauce
12. water
13. also
14. because
15. mall
16. daughter

Jesus, Mary, Joseph, I love You. Save souls!

J.M.J.

The Three Kings saw Baby Jesus.

J.M.J.

The angel told Mary to name her Son Jesus.

LESSON 8

/uh/ sound in us

butter
country
above
begun
love
bunch
son
sometimes
number
other
mother
sunny
another
under
until

BONUS

enough

J.M.J. Week Eight: Day 1

The **/uh/** sound in **u**s is usually spelled **u**, **ou**, or **o**.

A **Sort by Spelling**
Each box below has a different spelling of the **/uh/** sound in **u**s. On each line, write a list word that has the same spelling of this sound as the one in the box.

u	_____
	_____
	_____
	_____
	_____
	_____
ou	_____
o	_____
	_____
	_____
	_____
	_____
	_____
	_____

Jesus, Mary, Joseph, I love You. Save souls!

B **Complete the Sentence**
Starting with the first sentence, find the list word that completes the sentence. Write the word in the blank. Use each word only once.

1. During the _____ afternoon, we played in the shade.

2. The farmer made _____ from the cow's milk.

3. A _____ of grapes grew on the grapevine.

4. The angel told **Mary** to name her _____ Jesus.

5. Many families enjoy the fresh air in the _____.

6. Our house _____ is on our mailbox.

7. Timothy's _____ shoe is missing.

8. Mary is the _____ of God.

9. May I have _____ cookie, please?

10. John has _____ taking piano lessons.

11. _____ your neighbor as yourself.

12. The Christmas gifts were _____ the tree.

13. Remain at the table _____ you are excused.

14. The pope stood on the balcony _____ the people.

15. _____ we eat lunch at the park.

16. We have _____ food for everyone.

Week Eight: Day 3   J.M.J.

C Alphabetical Order

1.
2.
3.
4.
5.
6.
7.
8.
9.
10.
11.
12.
13.
14.
15.
16.

> **Tips** from your *Guardian Angel*
>
> - Ti**ll** is usually written with one **l** when it is added to another syllable, as in unti**l**.
> - The stressed /uh/ sound in **us** can be spelled with any vowel, as in **a**·go, it·**e**m, pen·c**i**l, at·**o**m, and cir·c**us**.

D Write the Homophone

sun

_____

E Write the Rhyming Words

1. dove

_____
_____

2. brother

_____
_____
_____

3. stuff

_____

4. fun

_____

F Write the Words with These Syllables

1. some

_____

2. sun

_____

3. but

_____

Jesus, Mary, Joseph, I love You. Save souls!

Pretest

J.M.J.　　　　　　　　　　　Week Eight: Day 4

Fold this page on the dotted line.
As you hear each dictated word, write it on the line.
When you are done, unfold the page and check your work.

1.
2.
3.
4.
5.
6.
7.
8.
9.
10.
11.
12.
13.
14.
15.
16.

1. butter
2. country
3. above
4. begun
5. love
6. bunch
7. son
8. sometimes
9. number
10. other
11. mother
12. sunny
13. another
14. under
15. until
16. enough

Jesus, Mary, Joseph, I love You. Save souls!

LESSON 9

J.M.J.

First Quarter Review

Lesson 1	Lesson 2	Lesson 3	Lesson 4
gone	pancake	cavity	letter
sew	grapevine	contact	bread
once	cannot	subtract	again
eye	homework	after	read
else	raindrop	rabbit	confess
is	paintbrush	napkin	any
only	grownup	answer	head
been	sidewalk	sandwich	many
from	backpack	Advent	spread
one	farmland	began	dead
quiet	sailboat	catfish	second
shall	bathtub	admit	Heaven
two	farmyard	animal	lesson
as	cowboy	branch	breakfast
shoe	playground	baptize	never
bonus laugh	**bonus** mousetrap	**bonus** Catholic	**bonus** telephone

Jesus, Mary, Joseph, I love You. Save souls!

J.M.J. Week Nine

Tips from your *Guardian Angel*

- Pronounce each word for correct spelling.
- Say the word, spell it, and say it again.
- Take an oral pretest of all these words, then write each misspelled word three times.

Lesson 5	Lesson 6	Lesson 7	Lesson 8
give	father	saw	butter
picture	upon	thought	country
pitcher	watch	often	above
minute	Amen	yawn	begun
hidden	wand	taught	love
hymnal	beyond	always	bunch
different	homily	soggy	son
myth	dollar	pause	sometimes
Indian	hurrah	awful	number
build	honor	awe	other
river	lot	sauce	mother
gypsy	wander	water	sunny
begin	koala	also	another
children	boxes	because	under
live	doctor	mall	until
bonus	**bonus**	**bonus**	**bonus**
America	apostle	daughter	enough

Jesus, Mary, Joseph, I love You. Save souls!

LESSON 10

/k/ as in cat, /s/ as in sat

scent
kitchen
kept
city
pencil
recess
cricket
circus
unique
balance
accept
scene
Christmas
catechism
except

BONUS

mosquito

Week Ten: Day 1

The /k/ sound in **c**at is spelled **c**, **ch**, **ck**, **k**, or **qu**. The /s/ sound in **s**at is usually spelled **s** or **c**, and sometimes it is spelled **sc**.

A Identify the Spelling

Each word below has a different spelling of the /k/ sound in **c**at or the /s/ sound in **s**at. Listen for these sounds as you pronounce each word.

Underline the spellings of the /k/ sound in **c**at.

c	circus	accept
	cricket	catechism
ch	Christmas	catechism
ck	cricket	
k	kitchen	kept
qu	unique	mosquito

Underline the spellings of the /s/ sound in **s**at.

s	recess	
	circus	mosquito
	Christmas	
c	city	accept
	pencil	except
	recess	balance
	circus	
sc	scent	scene

Jesus, Mary, Joseph, I love You. Save souls!

J.M.J.   Week Ten: Day 2

B Complete the Sentence
Starting with the first sentence, find the list word that completes the sentence. Write the word in the blank. Use each word only once.

1. Michael heard a _____ chirping in the grass.

2. On _____, we celebrate the birth of Jesus Christ.

3. Laura helps Mother cook in the _____.

4. I study my _____ lessons every day.

5. Each of us is a _____ person created by God.

6. We decided to _____ her invitation to the picnic.

7. All of us can swim _____ the baby.

8. Thomas _____ his workbooks in his desk.

9. The homeschooling family went to _____ museum.

10. The _____ of roses reminds me of Our Lady.

11. We saw an elephant at the _____.

12. The police arrived at the _____ of the accident.

13. I sharpen my _____ before taking a test.

14. Mom says we can play during _____, after lunch.

15. Billy kept his _____ and did not fall.

16. I heard a _____ buzzing around my head.

Jesus, Mary, Joseph, I love You. Save souls!

Week Ten: Day 3 — J.M.J.

C Alphabetical Order

1. _____
2. _____
3. _____
4. _____
5. _____
6. _____
7. _____
8. _____
9. _____
10. _____
11. _____
12. _____
13. _____
14. _____
15. _____
16. _____

> **Tips** from your *Guardian Angel*
>
> - The /k/ sound in **c**at after a short vowel is spelled **ck**, as in qua**ck**, ne**ck**, qui**ck**, clo**ck**, and du**ck**.
> - The letter **c** before **e**, **i**, or **y** makes the /s/ sound, as in **c**ent, **c**ity, and **c**ycle. It makes the /k/ sound before **a**, **o**, and **u**, as in **c**at, **c**old, and **c**up.
> - The letter **x** usually makes the /ks/ sound, as in e**x**cept.

D Write the Homophones

1. cent, sent

   _____

2. seen

   _____

E Write the Rhyming Words

1. swept

   _____

   _____

2. kitty

   _____

F Write the Words with These Syllables

1. pen

   _____

2. cat

   _____

3. Christ

   _____

Jesus, Mary, Joseph, I love You. Save souls!

Pretest

J.M.J. Week Ten: Day 4

Fold this page on the dotted line.
As you hear each dictated word, write it on the line.
When you are done, unfold the page and check your work.

1. scent
2. kitchen
3. kept
4. city
5. pencil
6. recess
7. cricket
8. circus
9. unique
10. balance
11. accept
12. scene
13. Christmas
14. catechism
15. except
16. mosquito

Jesus, Mary, Joseph, I love You. Save souls!

J.M.J.

Jesus was born on the first Christmas Day.

J.M.J.

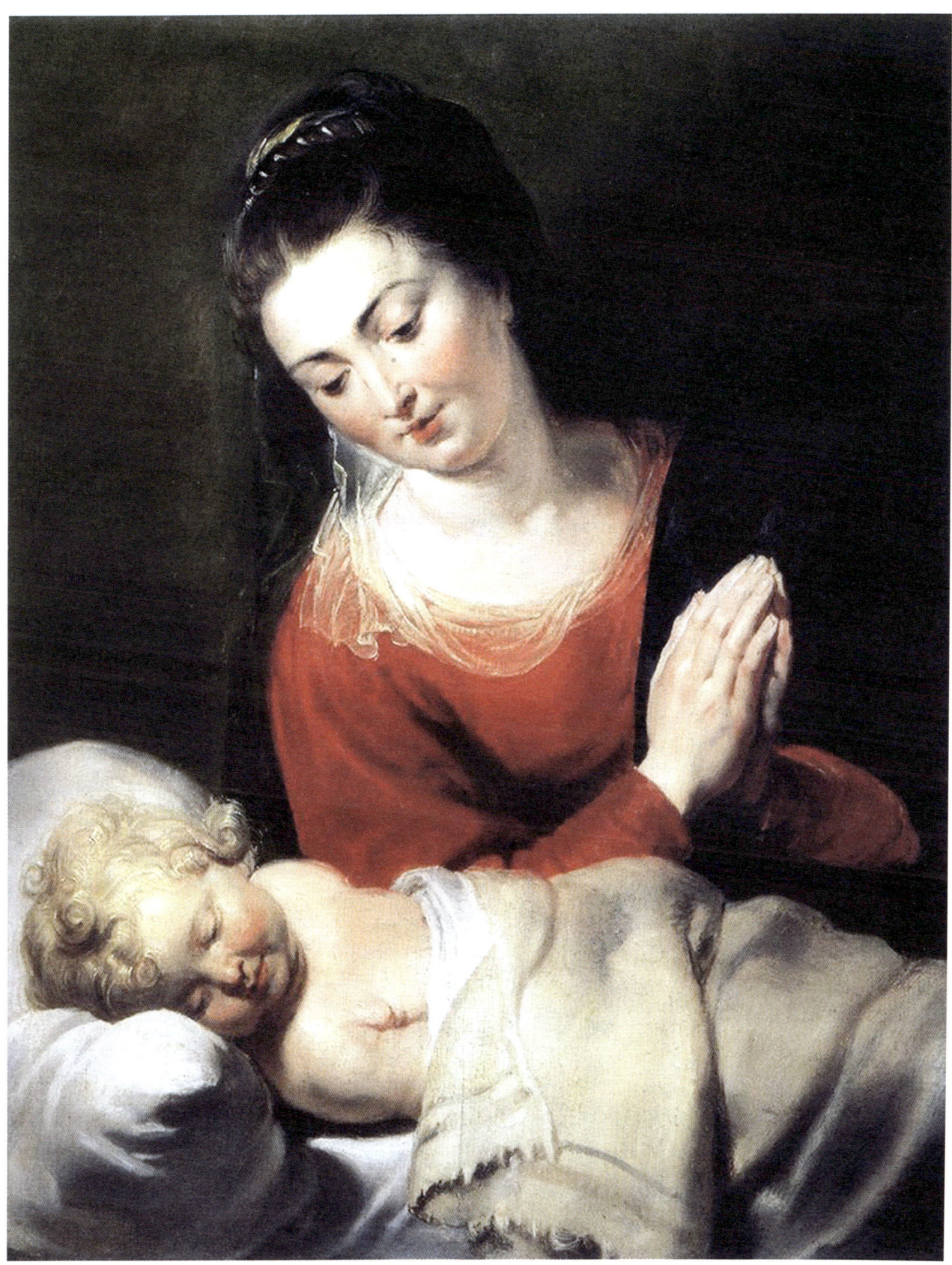

Gentle Jesus, meek and mild, look upon a little child.

LESSON 11

J.M.J.   Week Eleven: Day 1

/j/ as in jam, /z/ as in zoo

List words:
- gentle
- sneeze
- zero
- these
- gym
- fudge
- Jim
- close
- change
- badge
- please
- cheese
- scissors
- tragic
- those

BONUS
- xylophone

The **/j/** sound in **j**am is usually spelled **j**, **dge**, or **g**.
The **/z/** sound in **z**oo is usually spelled **z**, **s**, or **x**.

A. Sort by Spelling

Each box below has a different spelling of the **/j/** sound in jam or the **/z/** sound in zoo. On each line, write a list word that has the same spelling as the one in the box.

j	
dge	
g	
z	
s	
x	

B **Complete the Sentence**

Starting with the first sentence, find the list word that completes the sentence. Write the word in the blank. Use each word only once.

1. John threw the football to _____.

2. The children played basketball in the _____.

3. The doctor's photograph was on his identity _____.

4. Mom gave us _____ for a treat.

5. May I have a cookie, _____?

6. The plane crash was a _____ accident.

7. Please _____ your clothes before playing outside.

8. The losing team had _____ points.

9. The hymn began, "_____ Jesus, meek and mild."

10. Allergies make Susan _____.

11. Mice like to eat _____.

12. Please _____ the church door.

13. Use _____ to cut out the paper angel.

14. Give the red crayons to _____ children here.

15. Give the blue crayons to _____ children over there.

16. Jerome plays music on the _____.

Week Eleven: Day 3   J.M.J.

C Alphabetical Order

1.
2.
3.
4.
5.
6.
7.
8.
9.
10.
11.
12.
13.
14.
15.
16.

Tips from your *Guardian Angel*

- The letter **g** before **e, i,** or **y** sometimes makes the **/j/** sound, as in **g**em, **g**iant, and **g**ym. It usually makes the **/g/** sound before **a, o,** and **u,** as in **g**ame, **G**od, and **g**um.
- The **/j/** sound in **j**am after a short vowel is spelled **dge**, as in ba**dge**, le**dge**, ri**dge**, lo**dge**, and ju**dge**.
- The **/z/** sound in **z**oo at the beginning of a root word is usually spelled **z**, and never spelled **s**.

D Write the Homophones

1. Jim
2. clothes

E Write the Rhyming Words

1. judge
2. hose
3. bees
4. hero
5. strange

Pretest

J.M.J. Week Eleven: Day 4

Fold this page on the dotted line.
As you hear each dictated word, write it on the line.
When you are done, unfold the page and check your work.

1. _____ 1. gentle
2. _____ 2. sneeze
3. _____ 3. zero
4. _____ 4. these
5. _____ 5. gym
6. _____ 6. fudge
7. _____ 7. Jim
8. _____ 8. close
9. _____ 9. change
10. _____ 10. badge
11. _____ 11. please
12. _____ 12. cheese
13. _____ 13. scissors
14. _____ 14. tragic
15. _____ 15. those
16. _____ 16. xylophone

Jesus, Mary, Joseph, I love You. Save souls!

LESSON 12

Silent consonants

gnat
debts
knot
half
lamb
whole
hymn
yolk
wrote
knock
rhyme
hour
knife
ghost
kneel

BONUS

Psalms

J.M.J.　　　　　　　　　　Week Twelve: Day 1

> Silent consonants do not make a sound.

A Sort by Silent Letter
Each box below is labeled with a letter that is sometimes silent. On each line, write a list word that has the same silent consonant as the one in the box.

b	_____
g	_____
h	_____ _____
k	_____ _____ _____ _____ _____
l	_____ _____
n	_____
p	_____
w	_____

54　　　　　　　　　　　*Jesus, Mary, Joseph, I love You. Save souls!*

J.M.J.   Week Twelve: Day 2

B **Complete the Sentence**
Starting with the first sentence, find the list word that completes the sentence. Write the word in the blank. Use each word only once.

1. The Holy _____ is a name for the Holy Spirit.

2. We _____ during the Consecration of the Mass.

3. Soon, Grandma will arrive and _____ on the door.

4. A _____ is a very small insect.

5. The egg _____ is yellow.

6. Maria _____ a letter to her grandfather.

7. The hungry children ate the _____ pizza.

8. Daniel's job helps him to pay his _____.

9. The soft _____ slept close to the mother sheep.

10. Please untie the _____ in my shoelace.

11. Mother gave _____ of the apple to me.

12. The choir sang the _____ beautifully.

13. Listen to the _____ in the words *cat* and *sat*.

14. There are sixty minutes in an _____.

15. Be careful with that sharp _____!

16. King David wrote many of the _____ in the Bible.

Week Twelve: Day 3   J.M.J.

C Alphabetical Order

1.
2.
3.
4.
5.
6.
7.
8.
9.
10.
11.
12.
13.
14.
15.
16.

> **Tip** from your *Guardian Angel*
> Notice the silent letter as you practice writing the word. • • • • •

D Write the Homophones

1. yoke

2. rote

3. him

4. hole

5. rime

6. not

E Write the Rhyming Words

1. calf

2. ham

3. host

56   *Jesus, Mary, Joseph, I love You. Save souls!*

Pretest

J.M.J.

Week Twelve: Day 4

Fold this page on the dotted line.
As you hear each dictated word, write it on the line.
When you are done, unfold the page and check your work.

1.
2.
3.
4.
5.
6.
7.
8.
9.
10.
11.
12.
13.
14.
15.
16.

1. gnat
2. debts
3. knot
4. half
5. lamb
6. whole
7. hymn
8. yolk
9. wrote
10. knock
11. rhyme
12. hour
13. knife
14. ghost
15. kneel
16. Psalms

Jesus, Mary, Joseph, I love You. Save souls!

J.M.J.

King David wrote many of the Psalms and played them on his harp.

J.M.J.

Jesus gave a ring to Saint Catherine.

LESSON 13

/ng/ sound in si**ng**

ring
king
strong
long
bank
string
spring
sink
think
thank
wrong
thing
wing
bring
song

BONUS

young

Week Thirteen: Day 1

> The **/ng/** sound in si**ng** is usually spelled **ng**.
> Before **k**, it is spelled **n**, as in si**n**k.

A Sort by Spelling

Each box below has a different spelling of the **/ng/** sound in si**ng**. On each line, write a list word that has the same spelling as the one in the box.

ng	
n	

Week Thirteen: Day 2

B Complete the Sentence
Starting with the first sentence, find the list word that completes the sentence. Write the word in the blank. Use each word only once.

1. Before answering the question, _____ carefully.

2. Rebecca sang a _____ for her little sisters.

3. Mom wore a _____ dress to Mass.

4. Martha washed the dishes in the _____.

5. David played the harp for _____ Saul.

6. Samson was a _____ man.

7. Be sure to correct your _____ answers.

8. The _____ is a safe place to keep money.

9. Please _____ your rosary to church.

10. Forest animals drink water from a _____.

11. The kitten likes to play with a _____.

12. After receiving a gift, say, "_____ you."

13. A bird cannot fly with only one _____.

14. The _____ child stayed close to her mother.

15. What is that _____ over there?

16. Jesus gave a _____ to Saint Catherine.

Jesus, Mary, Joseph, I love You. Save souls!

Week Thirteen: Day 3 — J.M.J.

C Alphabetical Order

1.
2.
3.
4.
5.
6.
7.
8.
9.
10.
11.
12.
13.
14.
15.
16.

Tips from your *Guardian Angel*

- The **/ng/** sound in si**ng** alters the preceding vowel sound.
- The vowel sound that precedes **ng** or **nk** varies among different regional pronunciations.
- Note the irregular spelling of the vowel sound in y**ou**ng.

D Write the Homophone

wring

_____

E Write the Rhyming Words

1. sung

2. link

3. tank

4. tong

5. sting

J.M.J.   Week Thirteen: Day 4

Pretest

Fold this page on the dotted line.
As you hear each dictated word, write it on the line.
When you are done, unfold the page and check your work.

1. _____ 1. ring
2. _____ 2. king
3. _____ 3. strong
4. _____ 4. long
5. _____ 5. bank
6. _____ 6. string
7. _____ 7. spring
8. _____ 8. sink
9. _____ 9. think
10. _____ 10. thank
11. _____ 11. wrong
12. _____ 12. thing
13. _____ 13. wing
14. _____ 14. bring
15. _____ 15. song
16. _____ 16. young

Jesus, Mary, Joseph, I love You. Save souls!

LESSON 14

/ay/ sound in ate

break
they
vein
mail
pavement
away
weigh
mayor
paper
great
gray
crayon
eight
waste
obey

BONUS

favorite

J.M.J. Week Fourteen: Day 1

The **/ay/** sound in **a**te is usually spelled **a**, **ay**, **ai**, **eigh**, **ey**, **ea**, or **ei**.

A Sort by Spelling
Each box below has a different spelling of the **/ay/** sound in **a**te. On each line, write a list word that has the same spelling of this sound as the one in the box.

a	_____
	_____
	_____
	_____
ay	_____
	_____
	_____
	_____
ai	_____
eigh	_____
	_____
ey	_____
	_____
ea	_____
	_____
ei	_____

Jesus, Mary, Joseph, I love You. Save souls!

B **Complete the Sentence**
Starting with the first sentence, find the list word that completes the sentence. Write the word in the blank. Use each word only once.

1. The doctor took a blood sample from Mother's _____.

2. The poor children did not _____ their food.

3. The sky was _____ on the day Jesus died.

4. A birthday card arrived in the _____.

5. I am _____ years old.

6. _____ are my grandparents.

7. Did the baseball _____ that window?

8. Use a clean sheet of _____ for your spelling test.

9. God is _____.

10. How much do the tomatoes _____?

11. Our town elected a new _____.

12. Workers painted lines on the _____ in the parking lot.

13. Baptism takes _____ Original Sin.

14. I like to color with the red _____.

15. Jesus was happy to _____ His parents.

16. Chocolate ice cream is my _____ dessert.

Week Fourteen: Day 3 J.M.J.

C Alphabetical Order

1. _____
2. _____
3. _____
4. _____
5. _____
6. _____
7. _____
8. _____
9. _____
10. _____
11. _____
12. _____
13. _____
14. _____
15. _____
16. _____

Tips from your *Guardian Angel*

- The vowel **a** at the end of a syllable usually makes the /**ay**/ sound, as in p**a**·per.
- The /**ay**/ sound in **a**te is **not** spelled **a** at the end of root words.
- Divide before the consonant when a long vowel sound is followed by a consonant and another vowel, as in p**a**·per.

D Write the Homophones

1. ate _____
2. waist _____
3. brake _____
4. way _____
5. vain, vane _____
6. grate _____
7. male _____

Pretest

J.M.J.

Week Fourteen: Day 4

Fold this page on the dotted line.
As you hear each dictated word, write it on the line.
When you are done, unfold the page and check your work.

1.
2.
3.
4.
5.
6.
7.
8.
9.
10.
11.
12.
13.
14.
15.
16.

1. break
2. they
3. vein
4. mail
5. pavement
6. away
7. weigh
8. mayor
9. paper
10. great
11. gray
12. crayon
13. eight
14. waste
15. obey
16. favorite

Jesus, Mary, Joseph, I love You. Save souls!

J.M.J.

Jesus was happy to obey His parents.

J.M.J.

On Easter Sunday, Jesus rose from the dead.

LESSON 15

/ee/ sound in eve

really
even
between
study
carry
every
movie
key
daily
radio
Easter
lonely
relief
very
family

BONUS

priest

J.M.J. Week Fifteen: Day 1

The **/ee/** sound in **e**ve is usually spelled **e**, **ea**, **ee**, **ey**, **y**, **i**, or **ie**.

A Sort by Spelling

Each box below has a different spelling of the **/ee/** sound in **e**ve. On each line, write a list word that has the same spelling of this sound as the one in the box. Use each word only once.

e	
ea	
ee	
ey	
y	
i	
ie	

70

Jesus, Mary, Joseph, I love You. Save souls!

B Complete the Sentence

Starting with the first sentence, find the list word that completes the sentence. Write the word in the blank. Use each word only once.

1. On _____ Sunday, Jesus rose from the dead.

2. _____ your catechism questions.

3. Mother cut the birthday cake into _____ pieces.

4. My little sister slept _____ her two stuffed animals.

5. Dominic has been _____ good.

6. Dad listened to music on the _____.

7. We like to eat popcorn while watching a _____.

8. I _____ my rosary everywhere I go.

9. We read a saint's story _____ day.

10. The whole _____ knelt while praying the Rosary.

11. Eat green vegetables _____.

12. Jesus is _____ present in the Holy Eucharist.

13. Maria hopes to visit her _____ grandmother.

14. The cool water was a _____ from the hot weather.

15. The _____ heard confessions every Saturday.

16. Prayer is the _____ to Heaven.

Week Fifteen: Day 3   J.M.J.

C Alphabetical Order

1.
2.
3.
4.
5.
6.
7.
8.
9.
10.
11.
12.
13.
14.
15.
16.

> **Tips** from your *Guardian Angel*
>
> - The vowel **e** at the end of a syllable usually makes the /ee/ sound in **e**ve, as in b**e**·gin.
> - The /ee/ sound in **e**ve after **c** is spelled **ei**, as in re·**ce**ive.

D Write the Rhyming Words

1. feast

2. Steven

3. belief

4. merry

5. only

E Write the Words with These Syllables

1. real

2. be

72   Jesus, Mary, Joseph, I love You. Save souls!

J.M.J.   Week Fifteen: Day 4

Pretest

Fold this page on the dotted line.
As you hear each dictated word, write it on the line.
When you are done, unfold the page and check your work.

1.   1. really
2.   2. even
3.   3. between
4.   4. study
5.   5. carry
6.   6. every
7.   7. movie
8.   8. key
9.   9. daily
10.   10. radio
11.   11. Easter
12.   12. lonely
13.   13. relief
14.   14. very
15.   15. family
16.   16. priest

Jesus, Mary, Joseph, I love You. Save souls!

LESSON 16

J.M.J.

Week Sixteen: Day 1

> The **/iy/** sound in **ice** is usually spelled **i**, **ie**, **igh**, **y**, or **ui**.

/iy/ sound in ice

might
light
high
private
write
while
right
tiger
buy
sight
idea
guide
like
die
night

BONUS

identify

A. Sort by Spelling

Each box below has a different spelling of the **/iy/** sound in **ice**. On each line, write a list word that has the same spelling of this sound as the one in the box.

i	_____
	_____
	_____
	_____
	_____
ie	_____
igh	_____
	_____
	_____
	_____
i and y	_____
ui	_____
Sight word	_____

Jesus, Mary, Joseph, I love You. Save souls!

B **Complete the Sentence**
Starting with the first sentence, find the list word that completes the sentence. Write the word in the blank. Use each word only once.

1. Thomas saw a _____ at the zoo.

2. Sarah had a _____ talk with Father Brown.

3. Can you reach that _____ shelf?

4. Before going to sleep, I turn off the _____.

5. The bishop _____ visit our parish.

6. Jesus came to _____ for our sins.

7. Our guardian angel will _____ us through life.

8. Does Grandpa _____ my drawing of the angel?

9. Father David gives his blessing with his _____ hand.

10. I must _____ a thank-you letter to Sister Agnes.

11. Mother goes to the grocery store to _____ food.

12. The storm lasted all _____ long.

13. Sue laughed _____ Mr. Jones told the story.

14. Our Lord gave _____ to the blind man.

15. I have no _____ where I left my hat.

16. _____ the syllables in the spelling words.

Week Sixteen: Day 3   J.M.J.

C Alphabetical Order

1.
2.
3.
4.
5.
6.
7.
8.
9.
10.
11.
12.
13.
14.
15.
16.

Tips from your *Guardian Angel*

- The vowel **i** often makes the **/iy/** sound in **i**ce when it is followed by two consonants, as in k**i**nd.
- The vowels **i** and **y** at the end of a syllable sometimes make the **/ih/** sound in **i**t, as in fam·**i**·ly and bi·**cy**·cle, but they usually make the **/iy/** sound in **i**ce or the **/ee/** sound in **e**ve, as in ra·d**i**·o, wind·**y**, and f**i**·nal.

D Write the Homophones

1. by

2. hi

3. dye

4. rite

5. site

6. knight

7. mite

Pretest

J.M.J.

Week Sixteen: Day 4

Fold this page on the dotted line.
As you hear each dictated word, write it on the line.
When you are done, unfold the page and check your work.

1.
2.
3.
4.
5.
6.
7.
8.
9.
10.
11.
12.
13.
14.
15.
16.

1. might
2. light
3. high
4. private
5. write
6. while
7. right
8. tiger
9. buy
10. sight
11. idea
12. guide
13. like
14. die
15. night
16. identify

Jesus, Mary, Joseph, I love You. Save souls!

77

J.M.J.

Our Lord gave sight to the blind man.

J.M.J.

Mary stood below the Cross, weeping for Jesus.

LESSON 17

J.M.J.   Week Seventeen: Day 1

> The /**oh**/ sound in **o**ak is usually spelled **o, ow, ough,** or **oa.**

/oh/ sound in oak

window
dough
over
groan
follow
below
almost
open
knows
notice
yellow
own
rose
holy
owe

BONUS

though

A Sort by Spelling

Each box below has a different spelling of the /**oh**/ sound in **o**ak. On each line, write a list word that has the same spelling of this sound as the one in the box.

o	_____ _____ _____ _____ _____ _____
ow	_____ _____ _____ _____ _____ _____
ough	_____ _____
oa	_____

Jesus, Mary, Joseph, I love You. Save souls!

J.M.J. Week Seventeen: Day 2

B Complete the Sentence

Starting with the first sentence, find the list word that completes the sentence. Write the word in the blank. Use each word only once.

1. John _____ caught the ball, but he dropped it.

2. God _____ everything.

3. I watched the bread _____ rise in the warm oven.

4. Mary stood _____ the Cross, weeping for Jesus.

5. Saint Ann is pictured in the stained-glass _____.

6. I picked a _____ tulip.

7. The bridge crossed _____ the river.

8. A _____ was heard from the sick man's lips.

9. A _____ person is a happy one.

10. At Lourdes, Mary had a _____ on each foot.

11. _____ Mom, so that you won't get lost.

12. Alex put his _____ money in the church basket.

13. Did you _____ the name of that church?

14. Mother's door was _____.

15. Pay back what you _____ to others.

16. Grandma looked well, _____ she was ill.

Jesus, Mary, Joseph, I love You. Save souls!

Week Seventeen: Day 3   J.M.J.

C Alphabetical Order

1.
2.
3.
4.
5.
6.
7.
8.
9.
10.
11.
12.
13.
14.
15.
16.

Tips from your *Guardian Angel*

- The vowel **o** often makes the /oh/ sound in **o**ak when it is followed by two consonants, as in g**o**ld.
- The /oh/ sound in **o**ak can also be spelled **oe**, as in d**oe**.

D Write the Homophones

1. wholly

2. grown

3. doe

4. rows

5. oh

6. nose

E Write the Word with This Syllable

most

Pretest

J.M.J. Week Seventeen: Day 4

Fold this page on the dotted line.
As you hear each dictated word, write it on the line.
When you are done, unfold the page and check your work.

1.
2.
3.
4.
5.
6.
7.
8.
9.
10.
11.
12.
13.
14.
15.
16.

1. window
2. dough
3. over
4. groan
5. follow
6. below
7. almost
8. open
9. knows
10. notice
11. yellow
12. own
13. rose
14. holy
15. owe
16. though

Jesus, Mary, Joseph, I love You. Save souls!

LESSON 18

J.M.J.

Second Quarter Review

Lesson 10	Lesson 11	Lesson 12	Lesson 13
scent	gentle	gnat	ring
kitchen	sneeze	debts	king
kept	zero	knot	strong
city	these	half	long
pencil	gym	lamb	bank
recess	fudge	whole	string
cricket	Jim	hymn	spring
circus	close	yolk	sink
unique	change	wrote	think
balance	badge	knock	thank
accept	please	rhyme	wrong
scene	cheese	hour	thing
Christmas	scissors	knife	wing
catechism	tragic	ghost	bring
except	those	kneel	song
bonus	**bonus**	**bonus**	**bonus**
mosquito	xylophone	Psalms	young

Jesus, Mary, Joseph, I love You. Save souls!

J.M.J.   Week Eighteen

> **Tips** from your *Guardian Angel*
>
> - Pronounce each word for correct spelling.
> - Say the word, spell it, and say it again.
> - Take an oral pretest of all these words, then write each misspelled word three times.

Lesson 14	Lesson 15	Lesson 16	Lesson 17
break	really	might	window
they	even	light	dough
vein	between	high	over
mail	study	private	groan
pavement	carry	write	follow
away	every	while	below
weigh	movie	right	almost
mayor	key	tiger	open
paper	daily	buy	knows
great	radio	sight	notice
gray	Easter	idea	yellow
crayon	lonely	guide	own
eight	relief	like	rose
waste	very	die	holy
obey	family	night	owe
bonus favorite	**bonus** priest	**bonus** identify	**bonus** though

Jesus, Mary, Joseph, I love You. Save souls!

LESSON 19

J.M.J.

Week Nineteen: Day 1

The **/yoo/** sound in **u**se is usually spelled **u** or **ew**.

/yoo/ sound in use

beauty
usual
unit
unite
cubic
use
confuse
nephew
menu
refuse
humor
music
rescue
future
human

BONUS

uniform

A Sort by Spelling

Each box below has a different spelling of the **/yoo/** sound in **u**se. On each line, write a list word that has the same spelling of this sound as the one in the box.

u	
ue	
ew	
Sight word	

86

Jesus, Mary, Joseph, I love You. Save souls!

B **Complete the Sentence**

Starting with the first sentence, find the list word that completes the sentence. Write the word in the blank. Use each word only once.

1. Father John wrote the _____ for the hymn.

2. Uncle Bill took his niece and _____ to Mass.

3. Only God knows the _____.

4. Be careful when you _____ a knife.

5. Having too many choices might _____ you.

6. Always _____ candy from strangers.

7. My uncle tells his jokes with fun and good _____.

8. Jesus is both _____ and divine.

9. May I see the dinner _____?

10. We recognized the nurse by her _____.

11. The fireman climbed a tree to _____ the kitten.

12. We had the _____ amount of rain this past spring.

13. A pure soul has the greatest _____.

14. St. Josaphat tried to _____ his people.

15. An inch is a _____ of measurement.

16. An ice cube can be measured in _____ centimeters.

Week Nineteen: Day 3 J.M.J.

C Alphabetical Order

1. _____
2. _____
3. _____
4. _____
5. _____
6. _____
7. _____
8. _____
9. _____
10. _____
11. _____
12. _____
13. _____
14. _____
15. _____
16. _____

> **Tips** from your *Guardian Angel*
>
> - The vowel **u** at the end of a syllable usually makes the **/yoo/** sound in **u**se, as in **u**nit.
> - Most words do not end with the letter **u**, as in men**u**. Usually, a silent **e** is added to the **u**, as in res·**cue**.
> - The **/yoo/** sound in **u**se can also be spelled **eu**, as in f**eu**d.

D Write the Rhyming Words

1. rumor
   _____

2. suture
   _____

3. you
   _____
   _____
   _____

4. cutie
   _____

E Write the Words with These Syllables

1. fuse
   _____
   _____

2. form
   _____

3. man
   _____

Pretest

J.M.J.

Week Nineteen: Day 4

Fold this page on the dotted line.
As you hear each dictated word, write it on the line.
When you are done, unfold the page and check your work.

1.
2.
3.
4.
5.
6.
7.
8.
9.
10.
11.
12.
13.
14.
15.
16.

1. beauty
2. usual
3. unit
4. unite
5. cubic
6. use
7. confuse
8. nephew
9. menu
10. refuse
11. humor
12. music
13. rescue
14. future
15. human
16. uniform

Jesus, Mary, Joseph, I love You. Save souls!

J.M.J.

Jesus is both human and divine.

J.M.J.

Jesus knew He would die on the Cross.

LESSON 20

/ooh/ sound in **oo**ze

screw
group
into
rule
new
fruit
stew
statue
move
knew
school
zoo
neutral
truth
cocoon

BONUS

through

J.M.J. Week Twenty: Day 1

The **/ooh/** sound in **oo**ze is usually spelled
oo, **o**, **ew**, **ue**, **ui**, **ough**, **ou**, or **eu**.
Sometimes it is spelled **u**.

A Sort by Spelling

Each box below has a different spelling of the **/ooh/** sound in **oo**ze. On each line, write a list word that has the same spelling of this sound as the one in the box.

oo	_____
	_____
	_____
o	_____
	_____
ew	_____
	_____
	_____
	_____
ue	_____
ui	_____
ough	_____
ou	_____
eu	_____
u	_____

B **Complete the Sentence**
Starting with the first sentence, find the list word that completes the sentence. Write the word in the blank. Use each word only once.

1. A panda was born at the _____.

2. We will _____ into a bigger house.

3. Tighten the _____ in the cabinet.

4. I like to look at the _____ of Our Blessed Mother.

5. A _____ of geese is called a gaggle.

6. The boys went _____ the huge church.

7. The _____ is to be in bed by eight o'clock.

8. Gray is a _____ color.

9. A butterfly came out of the _____.

10. Jesus _____ He would die on the Cross.

11. We are enrolled in Seton Home Study _____.

12. I was excited when my _____ books arrived.

13. I like hot beef _____ on a chilly day.

14. Always tell the _____.

15. Melon is my favorite _____.

16. The yellow bus drove _____ the narrow tunnel.

Week Twenty: Day 3　　　J.M.J.

C Alphabetical Order

1. _____
2. _____
3. _____
4. _____
5. _____
6. _____
7. _____
8. _____
9. _____
10. _____
11. _____
12. _____
13. _____
14. _____
15. _____
16. _____

Tips from your *Guardian Angel*

- Memorizing the spelling of homophones can help you to remember the spelling patterns.
- Depending on the dialect, some homophones (such as **d**ew and **d**ue) may be pronounced with either the **/ooh/** sound in **oo**ze or the **/yoo/** sound in **u**se.

D Write the Homophones

1. gnu　_____
2. threw　_____

E Write the Rhyming Words

1. soup　_____
2. cool　_____
3. flute　_____
4. prove　_____
5. tooth　_____

Pretest

J.M.J.

Week Twenty: Day 4

Fold this page on the dotted line.
As you hear each dictated word, write it on the line.
When you are done, unfold the page and check your work.

1.
2.
3.
4.
5.
6.
7.
8.
9.
10.
11.
12.
13.
14.
15.
16.

1. screw
2. group
3. into
4. rule
5. new
6. fruit
7. stew
8. statue
9. move
10. knew
11. school
12. zoo
13. neutral
14. truth
15. cocoon
16. through

Jesus, Mary, Joseph, I love You. Save souls!

LESSON 21

/uu/ sound in book

sugar
pulpit
would
shook
hood
hook
butcher
could
wooden
bully
hooray
should
cookie
bushel
wool

BONUS

woodpecker

J.M.J.   Week Twenty-One: Day 1

The **/uu/** sound in b**oo**k is usually spelled **oo** or **u**. Sometimes it is spelled **ou**.

A **Sort by Spelling**
Each box below has a different spelling of the **/uu/** sound in b**oo**k. On each line, write a list word that has the same spelling of this sound as the one in the box.

oo	_____
	_____
	_____
	_____
	_____
	_____
	_____
u	_____
	_____
	_____
	_____
ou	_____
	_____
	_____

Jesus, Mary, Joseph, I love You. Save souls!

B **Complete the Sentence**
Starting with the first sentence, find the list word that completes the sentence. Write the word in the blank. Use each word only once.

1. Would you like to share my chocolate chip _____?

2. When Joseph _____ the branch, the leaves fell.

3. We need _____ to make the icing.

4. The brothers played with the _____ blocks.

5. Mom is knitting a _____ sweater for me.

6. The monk's _____ covered his face.

7. Mike caught a fish on the _____.

8. _____! The parade is passing by!

9. My sister and I picked a _____ of peaches.

10. The _____ cut the meat.

11. Tim was not frightened by the _____.

12. The priest preached from the _____.

13. We _____ obey our parents.

14. Peter certainly _____ beat me in chess.

15. _____ you peel an apple for me, please?

16. The _____ has black and red feathers.

Week Twenty-One: Day 3 J.M.J.

C Alphabetical Order

1. _____
2. _____
3. _____
4. _____
5. _____
6. _____
7. _____
8. _____
9. _____
10. _____
11. _____
12. _____
13. _____
14. _____
15. _____
16. _____

> **Tip** from your *Guardian Angel*
>
> Usually the /uu/ sound in b**oo**k followed by the /k/ sound in **c**at is spelled **ook**, as in c**ook**.

D Write the Homophone

wood

_____

E Write the Rhyming Words

1. good

   _____
   _____
   _____

2. book

   _____
   _____
   _____

F Write the Words with These Syllables

1. cook

   _____

2. bush

   _____

3. wood

   _____

4. ray

   _____

5. pit

   _____

Jesus, Mary, Joseph, I love You. Save souls!

Pretest

J.M.J.

Week Twenty-One: Day 4

Fold this page on the dotted line.
As you hear each dictated word, write it on the line.
When you are done, unfold the page and check your work.

1.
2.
3.
4.
5.
6.
7.
8.
9.
10.
11.
12.
13.
14.
15.
16.

1. sugar
2. pulpit
3. would
4. shook
5. hood
6. hook
7. butcher
8. could
9. wooden
10. bully
11. hooray
12. should
13. cookie
14. bushel
15. wool
16. woodpecker

Jesus, Mary, Joseph, I love You. Save souls!

J.M.J.

Saint Peter preached from the pulpit.

In this painting by Hans von Kulmbach (1485–1522), St. Peter is shown preaching to a German congregation. It was not unusual for an artist to place historic figures in the artist's own time period.

J.M.J.

God created the Earth and the other planets.

LESSON 22

/uhr/ sound in urn

urn
berth
person
earn
learn
worldwide
worry
furnace
squirm
early
workbook
hurry
earth
birthday
earthquake

BONUS

journey

J.M.J.   Week Twenty-Two: Day 1

The **/uhr/** sound in **ur**n is usually spelled **ur**, **er**, **ir**, **or**, or **ear**.

A Sort by Spelling

Each box below has a different spelling of the **/uhr/** sound in **ur**n. On each line, write a list word that has the same spelling of this sound as the one in the box.

ur	_____ _____ _____
er	_____ _____
ir	_____ _____
or	_____ _____
ear	_____ _____ _____ _____
Sight word	_____

Jesus, Mary, Joseph, I love You. Save souls!

B **Complete the Sentence**

Starting with the first sentence, find the list word that completes the sentence. Write the word in the blank. Use each word only once.

1. Children _____ good grades by studying.

2. Please _____, Larry. We might be late!

3. God the created the _____ and the other planets.

4. Christina wants to _____ how to play the piano.

5. Father Barrett was the only _____ in the room.

6. The _____ caused the bridge to fall.

7. The red icing on the cake spelled "Happy _____."

8. The _____ keeps our house warm in the winter.

9. Peggy, please do not _____ while you study.

10. The _____ bird catches the worm.

11. Write neatly in your _____, Richard.

12. The Catholic Church is a _____ religion.

13. Do not _____ about what you will eat.

14. The priest went on a _____ to Rome.

15. Mother put the pretty _____ in the living room.

16. Each sailor slept in a _____ on the ship.

Week Twenty-Two: Day 3 — J.M.J.

C Alphabetical Order

1. _____
2. _____
3. _____
4. _____
5. _____
6. _____
7. _____
8. _____
9. _____
10. _____
11. _____
12. _____
13. _____
14. _____
15. _____
16. _____

> **Tips** from your *Guardian Angel*
>
> - The **/uhr/** sound in **ur**n is spelled **or** only after the letter **w**, as in w**or**d and w**or**k.
> - Remember that **q** and **u** always go together. The **u** is not included in the spelling pattern for the sound **/uhr/** in squ**ir**m.

D Write the Homophones

1. urn

   _____

2. birth

   _____

E Write the Words with These Syllables

1. earth

   _____

   _____

2. world

   _____

3. fur

   _____

4. birth

   _____

5. work

   _____

Jesus, Mary, Joseph, I love You. Save souls!

Pretest

J.M.J. Week Twenty-Two: Day 4

Fold this page on the dotted line.
As you hear each dictated word, write it on the line.
When you are done, unfold the page and check your work.

1.
2.
3.
4.
5.
6.
7.
8.
9.
10.
11.
12.
13.
14.
15.
16.

1. urn
2. berth
3. person
4. earn
5. learn
6. worldwide
7. worry
8. furnace
9. squirm
10. early
11. workbook
12. hurry
13. earth
14. birthday
15. earthquake
16. journey

LESSON 23

/ahr/ sound in ark

bargain
part
scar
guard
card
arm
heart
garden
hard
harvest
art
stars
charge
carpet
bark

BONUS

faraway

J.M.J. — Week Twenty-Three: Day 1

The **/ahr/** sound in **ar**k is usually spelled **ar**.
Sometimes it is spelled **ear**.

A Sort by Spelling

Each box below has a different spelling of the **/ahr/** sound in **ar**k. On each line, write a list word that has the same spelling of this sound as the one in the box. (**Note**: the **/g/** sound may be spelled **gu**, as in **gu**ard.)

ar

_____
_____
_____
_____
_____
_____
_____
_____
_____
_____
_____
_____
_____
_____

ear

_____

B **Complete the Sentence**
Starting with the first sentence, find the list word that completes the sentence. Write the word in the blank. Use each word only once.

1. Please vacuum the _____, Martha.

2. Anthony has a _____ from the injury.

3. Ann fell and broke her _____.

4. I made a rosary in _____ class for Aunt Betty.

5. Have you sent a birthday _____ to Uncle John?

6. The dog's _____ woke up the neighbors.

7. I shared _____ of my sandwich.

8. _____ your soul from sin, Veronica.

9. Give your _____ to Jesus.

10. Our _____ has tomato plants.

11. Chores are sometimes _____ work.

12. Farmers will _____ the corn.

13. At the big sale, there were _____ prices.

14. God made all the _____ in the sky.

15. Pilate could find no _____ against Jesus.

16. There was a _____ look in Julie's eyes.

Week Twenty-Three: Day 3 J.M.J.

C Alphabetical Order

1.
2.
3.
4.
5.
6.
7.
8.
9.
10.
11.
12.
13.
14.
15.
16.

Tips from your *Guardian Angel*

- Usually, the letter **a** between two consonants in a single syllable makes the **/aa/** sound in c**a**t. However, when the letter **a** is followed by the letter **r**, the vowel sound changes to the **/ahr/** sound in c**ar**.
- The letters **g** and **u** sometimes go together to make the **/g/** sound, as in **gu**ard. The **u** is not included in the spelling pattern for the **/ahr/** sound in gu**ar**d.

D Write the Rhyming Words

1. start

2. yard

3. large

4. park

5. pardon

5. car

E Write the Word with This Syllable

car

108   Jesus, Mary, Joseph, I love You. Save souls!

J.M.J. Week Twenty-Three: Day 4

Pretest

Fold this page on the dotted line.
As you hear each dictated word, write it on the line.
When you are done, unfold the page and check your work.

1.
2.
3.
4.
5.
6.
7.
8.
9.
10.
11.
12.
13.
14.
15.
16.

1. bargain
2. part
3. scar
4. guard
5. card
6. arm
7. heart
8. garden
9. hard
10. harvest
11. art
12. stars
13. charge
14. carpet
15. bark
16. faraway

Jesus, Mary, Joseph, I love You. Save souls!

J.M.J.

Pilate could find no charge against Jesus.

J.M.J.

St. James prayed for the holy souls.

LESSON 24

/ayr/ sound in air

bear
wear
scared
pair
square
stair
their
care
tear
stare
pear
air
chair
haircut
share

BONUS

prayer

J.M.J. Week Twenty-Four: Day 1

> The **/ayr/** sound in **air** is usually spelled **air**, **are**, **ear**, or **eir**.

A Sort by Spelling

Each box below has a different spelling of the **/ayr/** sound in **air**. On each line, write a list word that has the same spelling of this sound as the one in the box.

air	_____ _____ _____ _____ _____
are	_____ _____ _____ _____ _____
ear	_____ _____ _____ _____
eir	_____
Sight word	_____

Jesus, Mary, Joseph, I love You. Save souls!

B Complete the Sentence

Starting with the first sentence, find the list word that completes the sentence. Write the word in the blank. Use each word only once.

1. Andrew takes good _____ of his brothers.

2. Do not _____ your paper out of your notebook.

3. The _____ was full of smoke from the incense.

4. Michael got up and let Grandma sit in his _____.

5. _____ your best clothes to Mass.

6. I tripped while climbing the last _____.

7. It is not polite to _____.

8. We should _____ wrongs patiently.

9. I have a new _____ of shoes.

10. The _____ tree is full of fruit.

11. The thunder and lightning _____ me.

12. I will _____ my hymn book with you.

13. A _____ has four equal sides.

14. James said a _____ for the holy souls.

15. They left _____ holy cards on the table.

16. Sam went to the barber to get a _____.

Week Twenty-Four: Day 3   J.M.J.

C Alphabetical Order

1.
2.
3.
4.
5.
6.
7.
8.
9.
10.
11.
12.
13.
14.
15.
16.

Tips from your *Guardian Angel*

- Memorizing the spelling of homophones can help you to remember the spelling patterns.
- The word pr**ayer** is a sight word because it does not follow the spelling patterns for the /ayr/ sound in **air**.

D Write the Homophones

1. bare

2. where

3. there

4. pare

5. stair

E Write the Rhyming Word

shared

F Write the Word with This Syllable

hair

Pretest

J.M.J.

Week Twenty-Four: Day 4

Fold this page on the dotted line.
As you hear each dictated word, write it on the line.
When you are done, unfold the page and check your work.

1.
2.
3.
4.
5.
6.
7.
8.
9.
10.
11.
12.
13.
14.
15.
16.

1. bear
2. wear
3. scared
4. pair
5. square
6. stair
7. their
8. care
9. tear
10. stare
11. pear
12. air
13. chair
14. haircut
15. share
16. prayer

Jesus, Mary, Joseph, I love You. Save souls!

LESSON 25

J.M.J. Week Twenty-Five: Day 1

The **/eer/** sound in **ear** is usually spelled **ear**, **ere**, **eer**, **eir**, or **ier**.

/eer/ sound in **ear**

peer
pier
fierce
deer
here
tear
near
clear
pierce
year
hear
fear
earring
tier
dear

BONUS

weird

A Sort by Spelling

Each box below has a different spelling of the **/eer/** sound in **ear**. On each line, write a list word that has the same spelling of this sound as the one in the box.

ear	_____
	_____
	_____
	_____
	_____
	_____
ere	_____
eer	_____
	_____
eir	_____
ier	_____
	_____
	_____

116 Jesus, Mary, Joseph, I love You. Save souls!

B Complete the Sentence

Starting with the first sentence, find the list word that completes the sentence. Write the word in the blank. Use each word only once.

1. Shepherds protect their sheep from _____ wolves.

2. There are 365 days in a _____.

3. Our souls are very _____ to Jesus.

4. The _____ left its tracks in the snow.

5. The weather was _____ and dry.

6. _____ means "to look intently."

7. The boat docked at the _____.

8. A _____ rolled down the cheek of little Maria.

9. The only thing we should _____ is offending God.

10. Your guardian angel is always _____ you.

11. God always will _____ our prayers.

12. "Please come _____," said Mother to Tommy.

13. Aunt Martha lost an _____.

14. Tony made a silly, _____ face, and we all laughed.

15. We saved the top _____ of the cake.

16. A soldier used a lance to _____ Our Lord's side.

Week Twenty-Five: Day 3 J.M.J.

C Alphabetical Order

1.
2.
3.
4.
5.
6.
7.
8.
9.
10.
11.
12.
13.
14.
15.
16.

> **Tip** from your *Guardian Angel*
>
> Memorizing the spelling of homophones can help you to remember the spelling patterns.

D Write the Homophones

1. pier
2. deer
3. tier
4. hear

E Write the Rhyming Words

1. beard
2. pierce

F Write the Words with These Letters

ear

Pretest

J.M.J.

Week Twenty-Five: Day 4

Fold this page on the dotted line.
As you hear each dictated word, write it on the line.
When you are done, unfold the page and check your work.

1.
2.
3.
4.
5.
6.
7.
8.
9.
10.
11.
12.
13.
14.
15.
16.

1. peer
2. pier
3. fierce
4. deer
5. here
6. tear
7. near
8. clear
9. pierce
10. year
11. hear
12. fear
13. earring
14. tier
15. dear
16. weird

Jesus, Mary, Joseph, I love You. Save souls!

J.M.J.

A soldier used a lance to pierce Our Lord's side.

J.M.J.

The Bible tells the true story of Jonas and the whale.

LESSON 26

J.M.J.   Week Twenty-Six: Day 1

/ohr/ sound in oar

four
pour
more
before
or
short
sore
Lord
corn
ore
story
store
form
oar
for

BONUS

record

> The **/ohr/** sound in **oar** is usually spelled **oar**, **or**, **ore**, or **our**.

A Sort by Spelling

Each box below has a different spelling of the **/ohr/** sound in **oar**. On each line, write a list word that has the same spelling of this sound as the one in the box.

oar	
or	
ore	
our	

Jesus, Mary, Joseph, I love You. Save souls!

B **Complete the Sentence**
Starting with the first sentence, find the list word that completes the sentence. Write the word in the blank. Use each word only once.

1. Should I study math _____ history?

2. He used the _____ to row the boat.

3. The miners discovered large quantities of iron _____.

4. There are _____ Gospel writers.

5. Dad bought a rosary at the Catholic _____.

6. Clare was too _____ to light the blessed candles.

7. _____ the milk carefully, Anna.

8. Grandma has a _____ finger.

9. We made Christmas cookies in the _____ of angels.

10. We eat dinner _____ we say the Rosary.

11. The Bible tells the true _____ of Jonas and the whale.

12. We wrapped gifts _____ the poor children.

13. May I please have _____ peas, Daddy?

14. _____ Jesus Christ, Son of God, have mercy on me!

15. After the harvest, the farmer's family eats _____.

16. Our pastor will _____ the date of the Baptism.

Week Twenty-Six: Day 3   J.M.J.

C Alphabetical Order

1. _____
2. _____
3. _____
4. _____
5. _____
6. _____
7. _____
8. _____
9. _____
10. _____
11. _____
12. _____
13. _____
14. _____
15. _____
16. _____

> **Tip** from your *Guardian Angel*
>
> Some dictionaries use two different pronunciation symbols for the **/ohr/** sound in **oar**. If you pronounce the words **or**, **ore**, and **oar** with the same sound, then you only need one pronunciation symbol.

D Write the Homophones

1. or
   _____

2. fore
   _____

3. soar
   _____

4. pore
   _____

E Write the Rhyming Words

1. bored
   _____

2. sport
   _____

3. born
   _____

4. storm
   _____

Jesus, Mary, Joseph, I love You. Save souls!

Pretest

J.M.J.

Week Twenty-Six: Day 4

Fold this page on the dotted line.
As you hear each dictated word, write it on the line.
When you are done, unfold the page and check your work.

1. _____ 1. four
2. _____ 2. pour
3. _____ 3. more
4. _____ 4. before
5. _____ 5. or
6. _____ 6. short
7. _____ 7. sore
8. _____ 8. Lord
9. _____ 9. corn
10. _____ 10. ore
11. _____ 11. story
12. _____ 12. store
13. _____ 13. form
14. _____ 14. oar
15. _____ 15. for
16. _____ 16. record

Jesus, Mary, Joseph, I love You. Save souls!

Lesson 27

J.M.J.

Third Quarter Review

Lesson 19	Lesson 20	Lesson 21	Lesson 22
beauty	screw	sugar	urn
usual	group	pulpit	berth
unit	into	would	person
unite	rule	shook	earn
cubic	new	hood	learn
use	fruit	hook	worldwide
confuse	stew	butcher	worry
nephew	statue	could	furnace
menu	move	wooden	squirm
refuse	knew	bully	early
humor	school	hooray	workbook
music	zoo	should	hurry
rescue	neutral	cookie	earth
future	truth	bushel	birthday
human	cocoon	wool	earthquake
bonus	**bonus**	**bonus**	**bonus**
uniform	through	woodpecker	journey

Jesus, Mary, Joseph, I love You. Save souls!

J.M.J.　　　　　　　　　　　　　　　　　　　Week Twenty-Seven

Tips from your *Guardian Angel*

- Pronounce each word for correct spelling.
- Say the word, spell it, and say it again.
- Take an oral pretest of all these words, then write each misspelled word three times.

Lesson 23	Lesson 24	Lesson 25	Lesson 26
bargain	bear	peer	four
part	wear	pier	pour
scar	scared	fierce	more
guard	pair	deer	before
card	square	here	or
arm	stair	tear	short
heart	their	near	sore
garden	care	clear	Lord
hard	tear	pierce	corn
harvest	stare	year	ore
art	pear	hear	story
stars	air	fear	store
charge	chair	earring	form
carpet	haircut	tier	oar
bark	share	dear	for
bonus	**bonus**	**bonus**	**bonus**
faraway	prayer	weird	record

Jesus, Mary, Joseph, I love You. Save souls!

LESSON 28

J.M.J.   Week Twenty-Eight: Day 1

/ou/ sound in out

The **/ou/** sound in **ou**t is usually spelled **ou** or **ow**. Sometimes it is spelled **ough**.

A Sort by Spelling
Each box below has a different spelling of the **/ou/** sound in **ou**t. On each line, write a list word that has the same spelling of this sound as the one in the box.

mouse
flower
our
without
mountain
sound
sour
found
around
about
crowd
down
cloud
outside
thousand

BONUS

drought

ou	_____
	_____
	_____
	_____
	_____
	_____
	_____
	_____
	_____
	_____
ow	_____
	_____
	_____
ough	_____

Jesus, Mary, Joseph, I love You. Save souls!

B Complete the Sentence

Starting with the first sentence, find the list word that completes the sentence. Write the word in the blank. Use each word only once.

1. We went _____ to play ball with Robert.

2. Mother talked _____ my lessons.

3. Jesus fed a large _____ with a few loaves and fishes.

4. I hear the _____ of chirping birds.

5. We walked _____ the race track.

6. A cumulus _____ looks like a big, fluffy cotton ball.

7. The cat chased the field _____ out of the barn.

8. Come to _____ house for dinner.

9. The happy children slid _____ the slide.

10. Timothy was lost, but his mother _____ him.

11. That candy is not sweet, but rather is _____ .

12. The number after 999 is one _____ .

13. God spoke to Moses on the _____ .

14. I picked a _____ for my mother's vase.

15. We cannot be happy _____ God.

16. The _____ caused the lake to dry up.

Week Twenty-Eight: Day 3 J.M.J.

C Alphabetical Order

1.
2.
3.
4.
5.
6.
7.
8.
9.
10.
11.
12.
13.
14.
15.
16.

> **Tips** from your *Guardian Angel*
>
> - A root is a word part to which a prefix, suffix, or ending may be added to form a new word.
> - The spelling **ou** is usually used in the middle of a root, as in c**ou**nt. The spelling **ow** is often used at the end of a root, as in c**ow**.
> - The **h** in **h**our is silent.
> - The word th**ou**, which is used in the Bible, follows the spelling pattern for the /ou/ sound in **ou**t.

D Write the Homophones

1. hour
2. flour

E Write the Rhyming Words

1. house
2. proud
3. devout

F Write the Words with This Syllable

out

130

Jesus, Mary, Joseph, I love You. Save souls!

Pretest

J.M.J. Week Twenty-Eight: Day 4

Fold this page on the dotted line.
As you hear each dictated word, write it on the line.
When you are done, unfold the page and check your work.

1.
2.
3.
4.
5.
6.
7.
8.
9.
10.
11.
12.
13.
14.
15.
16.

1. mouse
2. flower
3. our
4. without
5. mountain
6. sound
7. sour
8. found
9. around
10. about
11. crowd
12. down
13. cloud
14. outside
15. thousand
16. drought

Jesus, Mary, Joseph, I love You. Save souls!

J.M.J.

Jesus fed a large crowd with five loaves and two fishes.

J.M.J.

Jesus rose from the dead on Easter Sunday.

LESSON 29

/oi/ sound in oil

soybean
moisture
noise
ointment
spoil
voyage
appoint
oyster
poison
avoid
rejoice
royal
annoy
foil
noisy

BONUS

embroider

J.M.J.   Week Twenty-Nine: Day 1

The **/oi/** sound in **oi**l is spelled **oi** or **oy**.

A Sort by Spelling
Each box below has a different spelling of the **/oi/** sound in **oi**l. On each line, write a list word that has the same spelling of this sound as the one in the box.

| oi | _____ |
| oy | _____ |

B Complete the Sentence

Starting with the first sentence, find the list word that completes the sentence. Write the word in the blank. Use each word only once.

1. Eating too many snacks can _____ your appetite.

2. The _____ room was filled with happy families.

3. On Easter Sunday, we _____ in the Resurrection.

4. We must try to _____ the near occasions of sin.

5. Jesus did _____ Saint Peter as the first pope.

6. The king and queen took their _____ family to Mass.

7. If you open an _____, you might find a pearl.

8. Mother applied _____ to Ken's wound.

9. A steamy shower creates _____ on the mirror.

10. The cat heard a _____ and jumped.

11. Please, do not _____ your little sister, Daniel.

12. They sailed in a ship on a _____ to America.

13. Farmers grow and sell the _____ crop.

14. Mom wrapped the potatoes in _____ to bake them.

15. My grandmother can _____ the design.

16. Sin is _____ to our souls.

Week Twenty-Nine: Day 3   J.M.J.

C Alphabetical Order

1. _____
2. _____
3. _____
4. _____
5. _____
6. _____
7. _____
8. _____
9. _____
10. _____
11. _____
12. _____
13. _____
14. _____
15. _____
16. _____

> **Tips** from your *Guardian Angel*
>
> - A root is a word part to which a prefix, suffix, or ending may be added to form a new word.
> - The spelling **oi** is usually used in the middle of a root, as in b**oi**l. The spelling **oy** is often used at the end of a root, as in b**oy**.

D Write the Rhyming Words

1. boil

   _____

2. boys

   _____

3. enjoy

   _____

4. choice

   _____

5. cloister

   _____

6. anoint

   _____

7. annoyed

   _____

8. appointment

   _____

Jesus, Mary, Joseph, I love You. Save souls!

Pretest

J.M.J.

Week Twenty-Nine: Day 4

> Fold this page on the dotted line.
> As you hear each dictated word, write it on the line.
> When you are done, unfold the page and check your work.

1. soybean
2. moisture
3. noise
4. ointment
5. spoil
6. voyage
7. appoint
8. oyster
9. poison
10. avoid
11. rejoice
12. royal
13. annoy
14. foil
15. noisy
16. embroider

Jesus, Mary, Joseph, I love You. Save souls!

LESSON 30

J.M.J. — Week Thirty: Day 1

/sh/ sound in sheep

The **/sh/** sound in **sh**eep is usually spelled **sh**. It can also be spelled **ti**, **si**, **ci**, or **ch**.

mission
fraction
position
direction
mansion
passion
nation
solution
equation
station
caution
section
option
action
machine

BONUS

special

A Sort by Spelling

Each box below has a different spelling of the **/sh/** sound in **sh**eep. On each line, write a list word that has the same spelling of this sound as the one in the box.

ti	_____
	_____
	_____
	_____
	_____
	_____
	_____
	_____
	_____
si	_____
	_____
	_____
ci	_____
ch	_____

B Complete the Sentence

Starting with the first sentence, find the list word that completes the sentence. Write the word in the blank. Use each word only once.

1. Quick _____ extinguished the fire.

2. Use _____ when crossing the street.

3. Our family prayed at each _____ of the Cross.

4. If you have an _____, you have a choice.

5. The second _____ of the test was more difficult.

6. The rich man lived in a _____ with many rooms.

7. Christ's suffering and death are called His _____.

8. Our _____ on Earth is to serve God.

9. America is one _____ under God.

10. One-fourth of an apple is a _____ of the whole.

11. The math _____ was easily solved.

12. Go in the right _____ to get to the church.

13. Parents have the _____ of authority in the home.

14. The _____ to the problem is quite simple.

15. Mom cleaned our clothes in the washing _____.

16. My mother bakes a cake on _____ occasions.

Week Thirty: Day 3 J.M.J.

C Alphabetical Order

1. _____
2. _____
3. _____
4. _____
5. _____
6. _____
7. _____
8. _____
9. _____
10. _____
11. _____
12. _____
13. _____
14. _____
15. _____
16. _____

> **Tips** from your *Guardian Angel*
>
> - When you hear the sound /**sh**/ at the beginning of a word or at the end of a syllable, use the spelling **sh**, as in **sh**ut and wi**sh**.
> - When you hear the sound /**sh**/ at the beginning of any syllable after the first one, use the spelling **ti**, **si**, or **ci**, as in frac**ti**on, man**si**on, and spe**ci**al. (The exception to this rule is the ending **ship**, as in friend**ship**.)
> - When the syllable or root word before the /**sh**/ sound ends in **s**, use the **si** spelling, as in mi**ssi**on and pa**ssi**on.
> - When **si** is preceded by a vowel, it makes the /**zh**/ sound in vi**si**on.

D Write the Words with These Root Words

Each word below is included as a root word within one of the list words. Write the correct list word on each line.

1. pass

   _____

2. direct

   _____

3. man

   _____

4. miss

   _____

5. opt

   _____

Jesus, Mary, Joseph, I love You. Save souls!

Pretest

J.M.J.

Week Thirty: Day 4

Fold this page on the dotted line.
As you hear each dictated word, write it on the line.
When you are done, unfold the page and check your work.

1.
2.
3.
4.
5.
6.
7.
8.
9.
10.
11.
12.
13.
14.
15.
16.

1. mission
2. fraction
3. position
4. direction
5. mansion
6. passion
7. nation
8. solution
9. equation
10. station
11. caution
12. section
13. option
14. action
15. machine
16. special

Jesus, Mary, Joseph, I love You. Save souls!

J.M.J.

Christ's suffering and death are called His Passion.

J.M.J.

Many people listened to Jesus speak.

LESSON 31

Ending -le sound in Bible

Bible
ankle
circle
fable
paddle
whistle
bottle
middle
little
candle
bubble
bicycle
table
example
people

BONUS

article

When the ending **-le** sound in Bi**ble** has its own syllable, it is usually spelled **le**.

A Sort by Syllable

Say each list word out loud. Write it on a line in the box that is labeled with the number of syllables in the word. Circle **le** at the end of each word.

2 syllables

_____
_____
_____
_____
_____
_____
_____
_____
_____
_____
_____
_____

3 syllables

_____
_____
_____

J.M.J. Week Thirty-One: Day 2

B Complete the Sentence
Starting with the first sentence, find the list word that completes the sentence. Write the word in the blank. Use each word only once.

1. On the third Sunday of Advent, light the pink _____.

2. During Mass, we hear readings from the _____.

3. The duck swam in the _____ of the pond.

4. Margaret sprained her _____ while skating.

5. Gregory blew a big _____ with the soapy water.

6. We set the _____ while Mom cooked dinner.

7. The small child sat on the _____ chair.

8. You must be a good _____ for your brother.

9. Draw a _____ around the correct answer.

10. Wear a helmet when riding your _____.

11. The story of the lion and the mouse is a _____.

12. Many _____ listened to Jesus speak.

13. The engineer blew the train _____.

14. Carry a _____ of water with you on a hot day.

15. Jim used a _____ to steer his canoe.

16. Not one _____ of clothing was left unfolded.

Jesus, Mary, Joseph, I love You. Save souls!

Week Thirty-One: Day 3   J.M.J.

C Alphabetical Order

1. _____
2. _____
3. _____
4. _____
5. _____
6. _____
7. _____
8. _____
9. _____
10. _____
11. _____
12. _____
13. _____
14. _____
15. _____
16. _____

> **Tip** from your *Guardian Angel*
>
> When a word ending in **-le** is preceded by a consonant, divide the last syllable before the consonant, as in can·**dle** or fa·**ble**.

D Write the Rhyming Words

1. stable _____

2. trouble _____

3. handle _____

4. riddle _____

5. steeple _____

6. particle _____

7. brittle _____

8. sample _____

9. icicle _____

10. saddle _____

J.M.J. Week Thirty-One: Day 4

Pretest

Fold this page on the dotted line.
As you hear each dictated word, write it on the line.
When you are done, unfold the page and check your work.

1.
2.
3.
4.
5.
6.
7.
8.
9.
10.
11.
12.
13.
14.
15.
16.

1. Bible
2. ankle
3. circle
4. fable
5. paddle
6. whistle
7. bottle
8. middle
9. little
10. candle
11. bubble
12. bicycle
13. table
14. example
15. people
16. article

Jesus, Mary, Joseph, I love You. Save souls!

LESSON 32

Plurals -s, -es

cherries
beliefs
sisters
wishes
heroes
berries
watches
brothers
gives
prayers
hobbies
angels
knives
wolves
radios

BONUS

sacraments

J.M.J.   Week Thirty-Two: Day 1

> Plurals are formed by adding **s** or **es** to the singular noun.

A Form the Plurals

Simply add *s* to most nouns.

1. angel + s = _____
2. sacrament + s = _____
3. prayer + s = _____
4. sister + s = _____
5. radio + s = _____
6. brother + s = _____
7. belief + s = _____

Add *es* to nouns ending with *ss, x, z, ch,* or *sh*.

8. wish + es = _____
9. watch + es = _____

Change *y* to *i* before adding *es* when a noun ends with *y* preceded by a consonant.

10. cherry + es = _____
11. berry + es = _____
12. hobby + es = _____

Sometimes change *f* or *fe* to *v* before adding *es* when a noun ends with *f* or *fe*.

13. wolf + es = _____
14. knife + es = _____

Add *es* to a noun ending with *o* preceded by a consonant (except for some musical terms, such as piano*s*).

15. hero + es = _____

The same rules for plurals of nouns apply to verbs in the present tense, third person, singular.

16. give + s = _____

148   *Jesus, Mary, Joseph, I love You. Save souls!*

B **Complete the Sentence**
Starting with the first sentence, find the list word that completes the sentence. Write the word in the blank. Use each word only once.

1. The two _____ wore pink dresses to Easter Mass.

2. Our family says _____ before meals and bedtime.

3. Our guardian _____ help keep us safe from harm.

4. The red _____ had pits.

5. The children picked _____ from the bushes.

6. Jerry's many _____ keep him busy.

7. Our two clock _____ wake us up and play music.

8. The saints are good _____ for children to imitate.

9. The three _____ were altar boys.

10. The parish _____ food to the poor families.

11. Keep the sharp _____ away from young children.

12. A good shepherd protects his sheep from _____.

13. I make special _____ on my birthday!

14. My parents know the time by looking at their _____.

15. Baptism and Confirmation are _____ .

16. We learn our Catholic _____ in the catechism.

Week Thirty-Two: Day 3   J.M.J.

C Alphabetical Order

1. _____
2. _____
3. _____
4. _____
5. _____
6. _____
7. _____
8. _____
9. _____
10. _____
11. _____
12. _____
13. _____
14. _____
15. _____
16. _____

> **Tip** from your *Guardian Angel*
>
> In the noun **belief**, the **f** does not change to a **v** in the plural form: **beliefs**. If it did change to a **v**, the noun would change to the verb **believes**.

D Write the Plurals

For each noun below, find the list word that is the plural form. Write the list word on the line.

1. radio

   _____

2. berry

   _____

3. belief

   _____

4. wolf

   _____

5. prayer

   _____

6. knife

   _____

7. hero

   _____

8. wish

   _____

Jesus, Mary, Joseph, I love You. Save souls!

J.M.J. Week Thirty-Two: Day 4

Pretest

Fold this page on the dotted line.
As you hear each dictated word, write it on the line.
When you are done, unfold the page and check your work.

1.
2.
3.
4.
5.
6.
7.
8.
9.
10.
11.
12.
13.
14.
15.
16.

1. cherries
2. beliefs
3. sisters
4. wishes
5. heroes
6. berries
7. watches
8. brothers
9. gives
10. prayers
11. hobbies
12. angels
13. knives
14. wolves
15. radios
16. sacraments

Jesus, Mary, Joseph, I love You. Save souls!

J.M.J.

Jesus is the Good Shepherd, Who protects His sheep.

J.M.J.

Saint Paul was famous for his preaching.

LESSON 33

Ending -ing

staying
preaching
praising
crying
fasting
going
walking
blessing
giving
floating
spelling
digging
praying
trusting
jumping

BONUS

forgetting

J.M.J.   Week Thirty-Three: Day 1

> The /ing/ sound in **ring** is spelled **ing**. We add the ending **-ing** to the end of a verb to change the meaning.

A Add the Ending -ing

Drop the silent *e* at the end of a word before adding a vowel suffix.

1. praise + ing = _____
2. give + ing = _____

Double the final consonant of a short-vowel, one-syllable word ending with one consonant before adding a vowel suffix.

3. dig + ing = _____

Usually, double the final consonant of a two-syllable word ending with one consonant before adding a vowel suffix.

4. forget + ing = _____

Simply add *-ing* to other verbs.

5. pray + ing = _____
6. stay + ing = _____
7. cry + ing = _____
8. preach + ing = _____
9. jump + ing = _____
10. go + ing = _____
11. trust + ing = _____
12. fast + ing = _____
13. spell + ing = _____
14. bless + ing = _____
15. walk + ing = _____
16. float + ing = _____

J.M.J.   Week Thirty-Three: Day 2

B **Complete the Sentence**
Starting with the first sentence, find the list word that completes the sentence. Write the word in the blank. Use each word only once.

1. Paul's toy sailboat was _____ on the water.

2. After lunch, we are _____ to the park.

3. I am _____ some of my toys to the poor children.

4. Dad is _____ the Rosary.

5. I check my words for correct _____.

6. We enjoy _____ after Mass to pray the Rosary.

7. The baby is _____ because she is hungry.

8. We will be _____ during Lent.

9. The farmers are _____ God to send rain.

10. St. Paul was famous for his _____ to the Romans.

11. The choir is _____ God by singing hymns.

12. We were _____ to church in the snow.

13. I saw my dog _____ in the dirt.

14. My cat was _____ over the toy.

15. Babies are a _____ from God.

16. Are you _____ about the novena tomorrow?

Jesus, Mary, Joseph, I love You. Save souls!

Week Thirty-Three: Day 3   J.M.J.

C Alphabetical Order

1. _____
2. _____
3. _____
4. _____
5. _____
6. _____
7. _____
8. _____
9. _____
10. _____
11. _____
12. _____
13. _____
14. _____
15. _____
16. _____

> **Tips** from your *Guardian Angel*
>
> - The word **worship** has two acceptable spellings for adding **-ing**. One spelling follows the rule: **worshipping**. The other spelling is an exception to the rule: **worshiping**.
> - When a suffix causes the stress to be moved to the first syllable of a word, do not double the final consonant (re·fer′, re·ferred′, ref′·er·ence).

D Write the Words with These Syllables

1. stay
   _____

2. preach
   _____

3. cry
   _____

4. walk
   _____

5. bless
   _____

6. spell
   _____

7. pray
   _____

J.M.J. Week Thirty-Three: Day 4

Pretest

Fold this page on the dotted line.
As you hear each dictated word, write it on the line.
When you are done, unfold the page and check your work.

1. staying
2. preaching
3. praising
4. crying
5. fasting
6. going
7. walking
8. blessing
9. giving
10. floating
11. spelling
12. digging
13. praying
14. trusting
15. jumping
16. forgetting

Jesus, Mary, Joseph, I love You. Save souls!

LESSON 34

Ending -ed

roasted
graded
framed
planned
cried
wanted
lived
started
tried
missed
praised
stayed
called
looked
kissed

BONUS

laughed

J.M.J. Week Thirty-Four: Day 1

> The ending -**ed** makes three different sounds: the /**d**/ sound in liv**ed**, the /**t**/ sound in miss**ed**, and the /**ed**/ sound in grad**ed**. We add the ending -**ed** to the end of a verb to change the meaning.

A Add the Ending -ed

Drop the silent *e* at the end of a word before adding a vowel suffix.

1. grade + ed = _____
2. frame + ed = _____
3. live + ed = _____
4. praise + ed = _____

Double the final consonant of a short-vowel, one-syllable word ending with one consonant before adding a vowel suffix.

5. plan + ed = _____

Change *y* to *i* before adding a suffix that does not begin with *i*.

6. cry + ed = _____
7. try + ed = _____

Simply add *-ed* to other verbs.

8. roast + ed = _____
9. kiss + ed = _____
10. want + ed = _____
11. laugh + ed = _____
12. start + ed = _____
13. miss + ed = _____
14. stay + ed = _____
15. look + ed = _____
16. call + ed = _____

B Complete the Sentence

Starting with the first sentence, find the list word that completes the sentence. Write the word in the blank. Use each word only once.

1. Uncle Steve _____ our family portrait.

2. Grandma _____ the chicken in the oven.

3. We came inside before the rain _____.

4. The family _____ God for His goodness.

5. God _____ Adam and Eve to be happy.

6. Thomas _____ in bed because he was sick.

7. Our sick baby brother _____ all night.

8. Mother _____ the doctor about our sick baby.

9. The Holy Family _____ in Nazareth.

10. The priest _____ through the old prayer book.

11. I _____ to spell all the words correctly.

12. My spelling test was _____ by my mom.

13. The devoted father _____ each child good night.

14. I _____ only one word on my last test.

15. The children _____ at the clown.

16. We _____ our trip to the cathedral.

Week Thirty-Four: Day 3 J.M.J.

C Alphabetical Order

1. _____
2. _____
3. _____
4. _____
5. _____
6. _____
7. _____
8. _____
9. _____
10. _____
11. _____
12. _____
13. _____
14. _____
15. _____
16. _____

Tip from your *Guardian Angel*

🕊 Past-tense words ending in **-ed** make the **/d/** sound or **/t/** sound when the root ends with a letter other than **d** or **t**; otherwise, the ending **-ed** makes the **/ed/** sound. • • • • • • • • •

D Sort by the Sound of the Suffix -ed

1. Write list words in which the suffix **-ed** makes the **/d/** sound.

   _____ _____

   _____ _____

   _____ _____

   _____ _____

2. Write list words in which the suffix **-ed** makes the **/t/** sound.

   _____ _____

   _____ _____

3. Write list words in which the suffix **-ed** makes the **/ed/** sound.

   _____ _____

   _____ _____

Pretest

J.M.J.

Week Thirty-Four: Day 4

Fold this page on the dotted line.
As you hear each dictated word, write it on the line.
When you are done, unfold the page and check your work.

1. roasted
2. graded
3. framed
4. planned
5. cried
6. wanted
7. lived
8. started
9. tried
10. missed
11. praised
12. stayed
13. called
14. looked
15. kissed
16. laughed

Jesus, Mary, Joseph, I love You. Save souls!

J.M.J.

God wanted Adam and Eve to be happy.

J.M.J.

Our Lord and His Blessed Mother give us their love.

LESSON 35

Suffixes -ly, -ful

finally
wonderful
annually
thankful
hourly
graceful
careful
beautifully
fatherly
friendly
weekly
monthly
motherly
faithfully
lively

BONUS

usually

J.M.J. Week Thirty-Five: Day 1

> We add the suffix **-ful** at the end of a word to form an adjective. We add the suffix **-ly** at the end of a word to form an adverb.

A Sort by Suffix

Each box below is labeled with a suffix. On each line, write a list word that has the same suffix as the one in the box.

-ful	_____ _____ _____ _____
-fully	_____ _____
-ly	_____ _____ _____ _____ _____ _____ _____ _____

Jesus, Mary, Joseph, I love You. Save souls!

B Complete the Sentence

Starting with the first sentence, find the list word that completes the sentence. Write the word in the blank. Use each word only once.

1. Our Blessed Mother gives us her _____ love.

2. God gives us His _____ love.

3. The _____ families talked after Mass.

4. The _____ children ran in the playground.

5. The new church was _____ opened.

6. Catholics enter the church _____ for adoration.

7. Catholics attend Sunday Mass _____.

8. First Friday devotions occur _____.

9. Christmas Day occurs _____.

10. I am _____ for my Catholic Faith.

11. Homeschooling is a _____ family activity.

12. The _____ ballerina danced on the stage.

13. Sister Agnes _____ keeps her vows.

14. The bride was dressed _____.

15. Be _____ when you cross the street.

16. It _____ is cold on Christmas Eve.

Week Thirty-Five: Day 3   J.M.J.

C Alphabetical Order

1. _____
2. _____
3. _____
4. _____
5. _____
6. _____
7. _____
8. _____
9. _____
10. _____
11. _____
12. _____
13. _____
14. _____
15. _____
16. _____

Tips from your *Guardian Angel*

- A base word is a word to which a prefix, suffix, or ending may be added to form a new word.
- A suffix is a word part that is added to the end of a base word to change the meaning.
- The suffix **-ful** means "full of." The suffix **-ly** forms an adverb and means "in a certain manner."
- Divide between the base word and the suffix.
- Ful**l** is usually written with one **l** when it is added to another syllable, as in carefu**l**.
- Learning the rules for dividing words into syllables, as well as the meanings of the suffixes, can help you to memorize the correct spelling.

D Write the Words with These Syllables

1. wonder
   _____
2. annual
   _____
3. beautiful
   _____
4. father
   _____
5. mother
   _____

Jesus, Mary, Joseph, I love You. Save souls!

Pretest

J.M.J.

Week Thirty-Five: Day 4

Fold this page on the dotted line.
As you hear each dictated word, write it on the line.
When you are done, unfold the page and check your work.

1.
2.
3.
4.
5.
6.
7.
8.
9.
10.
11.
12.
13.
14.
15.
16.

1. finally
2. wonderful
3. annually
4. thankful
5. hourly
6. graceful
7. careful
8. beautifully
9. fatherly
10. friendly
11. weekly
12. monthly
13. motherly
14. faithfully
15. lively
16. usually

Jesus, Mary, Joseph, I love You. Save souls!

J.M.J.

Fourth Quarter Review

Lesson 28	Lesson 29	Lesson 30	Lesson 31
mouse	soybean	mission	Bible
flower	moisture	fraction	ankle
our	noise	position	circle
without	ointment	direction	fable
mountain	spoil	mansion	paddle
sound	voyage	passion	whistle
sour	appoint	nation	bottle
found	oyster	solution	middle
around	poison	equation	little
about	avoid	station	candle
crowd	rejoice	caution	bubble
down	royal	section	bicycle
cloud	annoy	option	table
outside	foil	action	example
thousand	noisy	machine	people
bonus	**bonus**	**bonus**	**bonus**
drought	embroider	special	article

Jesus, Mary, Joseph, I love You. Save souls!

J.M.J.   Week Thirty-Six

> **Tips** from your *Guardian Angel*
>
> - Pronounce each word for correct spelling.
> - Say the word, spell it, and say it again.
> - Take an oral pretest of all these words, then write each misspelled word three times.

Lesson 32	Lesson 33	Lesson 34	Lesson 35
cherries	staying	roasted	finally
beliefs	preaching	graded	wonderful
sisters	praising	framed	annually
wishes	crying	planned	thankful
heroes	fasting	cried	hourly
berries	going	wanted	graceful
watches	walking	lived	careful
brothers	blessing	started	beautifully
gives	giving	tried	fatherly
prayers	floating	missed	friendly
hobbies	spelling	praised	weekly
angels	digging	stayed	monthly
knives	praying	called	motherly
wolves	trusting	looked	faithfully
radios	jumping	kissed	lively
bonus sacraments	**bonus** forgetting	**bonus** laughed	**bonus** usually

Jesus, Mary, Joseph, I love You. Save souls!

J.M.J.

Spelling 3 for Young Catholics

ALPHABETIZED WORD LIST

about	bathtub	care	dear	finally	half
above	bear	careful	debts	floating	hard
accept	beautifully	carpet	deer	flower	harvest
action	beauty	carry	die	foil	head
admit	because	catechism	different	follow	hear
Advent	been	catfish	digging	for	heart
after	before	Catholic	direction	forgetting	Heaven
again	began	caution	doctor	form	here
air	begin	cavity	dollar	found	heroes
almost	begun	chair	dough	four	hidden
also	beliefs	change	down	fraction	high
always	below	charge	drought	framed	hobbies
Amen	berries	cheese	early	friendly	holy
America	berth	cherries	earn	from	homework
angels	between	children	earring	fruit	homily
animal	beyond	Christmas	earth	fudge	honor
ankle	Bible	circle	earthquake	furnace	hood
annoy	bicycle	circus	Easter	future	hook
annually	birthday	city	eight	garden	hooray
another	blessing	clear	else	gentle	hour
answer	bottle	close	embroider	ghost	hourly
any	boxes	cloud	enough	give	human
apostle	branch	cocoon	equation	gives	humor
appoint	bread	confess	even	giving	hurrah
arm	break	confuse	every	gnat	hurry
around	breakfast	contact	example	going	hymn
art	bring	cookie	except	gone	hymnal
article	brothers	corn	eye	graceful	idea
as	bubble	could	fable	graded	identify
avoid	build	country	faithfully	grapevine	Indian
away	bully	cowboy	family	gray	into
awe	bunch	crayon	faraway	great	is
awful	bushel	cricket	farmland	groan	Jim
backpack	butcher	cried	farmyard	group	journey
badge	butter	crowd	fasting	grownup	jumping
balance	buy	crying	father	guard	kept
bank	called	cubic	fatherly	guide	key
baptize	candle	daily	favorite	gym	king
bargain	cannot	daughter	fear	gypsy	kissed
bark	card	dead	fierce	haircut	kitchen

Jesus, Mary, Joseph, I love You. Save souls!

kneel	mousetrap	pencil	sandwich	staying	very
knew	move	people	sauce	stew	voyage
knife	movie	person	saw	store	walking
knives	music	picture	scar	story	wand
knock	myth	pier	scared	string	wander
knot	napkin	pierce	scene	strong	wanted
knows	nation	pitcher	scent	study	waste
koala	near	planned	school	subtract	watch
lamb	nephew	playground	scissors	sugar	watches
laugh	neutral	please	screw	sunny	water
laughed	never	poison	second	table	wear
learn	new	position	section	taught	weekly
lesson	night	pour	sew	tear	weigh
letter	noise	praised	shall	tear	weird
light	noisy	praising	share	telephone	while
like	notice	prayer	shoe	thank	whistle
little	number	prayers	shook	thankful	whole
live	oar	praying	short	their	window
lived	obey	preaching	should	these	wing
lively	often	priest	sidewalk	they	wishes
lonely	ointment	private	sight	thing	without
long	once	Psalms	sink	think	wolves
looked	one	pulpit	sisters	those	wonderful
Lord	only	quiet	sneeze	though	wooden
lot	open	rabbit	soggy	thought	woodpecker
love	option	radio	solution	thousand	wool
machine	or	radios	sometimes	through	workbook
mail	ore	raindrop	son	tier	worldwide
mall	other	read	song	tiger	worry
mansion	our	really	sore	tragic	would
many	outside	recess	sound	tried	write
mayor	over	record	soybean	trusting	wrong
menu	owe	refuse	special	truth	wrote
middle	own	rejoice	spelling	two	xylophone
might	oyster	relief	spoil	under	yawn
minute	paddle	rescue	spread	uniform	year
missed	paintbrush	rhyme	spring	unique	yellow
mission	pair	right	square	unit	yolk
moisture	pancake	ring	squirm	unite	young
monthly	paper	river	stair	until	zero
more	part	roasted	stare	upon	zoo
mosquito	passion	rose	stars	urn	
mother	pause	royal	started	use	
motherly	pavement	rule	station	usual	
mountain	pear	sacraments	statue	usually	
mouse	peer	sailboat	stayed	vein	

Jesus, Mary, Joseph, I love You. Save souls!

Spelling Short Vowel Sounds

Vowel Sounds	Common Spelling Patterns	Sample Words	Some Other Spellings
/aa/ in at	a	at	au (laugh)
/eh/ in egg	e, ea	red, read	ai (said)
/ih/ in it	i, y, ui	him, hymn, build	ee (been)
/ah/ in ox	o, a	ox, Amen	ho (honor)
/uh/ in us	u, ou	us, touch	o (son)

Spelling Long Vowel Sounds

Vowel Sounds	Common Spelling Patterns	Sample Words	Some Other Spellings
/ay/ in ate	a, ay, ai, eigh, ey, ea, ei	ate, hay, rain, eight, hey, break, rein	eig (reign)
/ee/ in eve	e, ea, ee, ey, y, i, ie, ei	eve, sea, see, key, holy, piano, priest, receive	eo (people)
/iy/ in ice	i, ie, igh, y, ui	site, tie, sight, by, guide	uy (buy)
/oh/ in oak	o, ow, ough, oa, oe, oo, ou	so, grown, dough, groan, doe, floor, four	ew (sew)
/yoo/ in use	u, ew, eu	use, few, feud	eau (beauty)

Spelling Other Vowel Sounds

Vowel Sounds	Common Spelling Patterns	Sample Words	Some Other Spellings
/aw/ in awe	a, o, aw, au, ough	call, often, paw, pause, thought	augh (taught)
/ooh/ in ooze	oo, o, ew, ue, ui, ough, ou, eu	too, to, blew, blue, fruit, through, group, neutral	u (truth)
/uu/ in book	oo, u	wood, put	ou (would)
/ou/ in out	ou, ow	out, bow	ough (bough)
/oi/ in oil	oi, oy	oil, boy	

Spelling Consonant Sounds

Consonant Sounds	Common Spelling Patterns	Sample Words	Some Other Spellings
/b/ in bell	b	bell	bb (rabbit)
/d/ in dad	d, ed	dad, loved	dd (sudden)
/f/ in fan	f, ph, gh	fan, phone, laugh	ff (stuff)
/g/ in God	g, gh	God, ghost	gu (guard)
/h/ in hat	h	hole	wh (whole)
/j/ in jam	j, dge, g	jam, fudge, gem	ge (cage)
/k/ in cat	c, ch, ck, k	cat, school, duck, kitten	qu (mosquito)
/l/ in lamb	l	lamb	ll (mall)
/m/ in Mass	m	Mass	mb (lamb)
/n/ in nun	n, kn, gn	no, know, gnat	pn (pneumonia)
/p/ in pet	p	pet	pp (happen)
/kw/ in queen	qu	queen	cu (cuisine)
/r/ in run	r, wr	right, write	rh (rhyme)
/s/ in sat	s, c, sc	sent, cent, scent	ss (Mass)
/t/ in top	t, ed	top, fixed	tt (kitten)
/v/ in van	v	van	f (of)
/w/ in wise	w, wh	won, whale	o (one)
/ks/ in box	x	box	cks (rocks)
/y/ in yes	y	yes	i (onion)
/z/ in zoo	z, s	zoo, is	x (xylophone)
/ch/ in church	ch, tch	church, watch	ti (question)
/ng/ in sing	ng	sing	n (sink)
/sh/ in sheep	sh, ti, si, ci, ch	sheep, fraction, mission, special, machine	ce (ocean)
/th/ in this	th	this	
/th/ in thin	th	thin	
/zh/ in vision	si, ti	vision, equation	s (usual)

J.M.J.

SPELLING RULES FOR CONSONANTS

The **/kw/** sound is usually spelled with the two letters **q** and **u**, as in **qu**iet. The letter **q** is always followed by the letter **u**.

The **/l/**, **/f/**, and **/s/** sounds after a single vowel in one-syllable words are often spelled **ll**, **ff**, and **ss**, as in be**ll**, stu**ff**, and Ma**ss**.

The **/k/** sound after a short vowel is spelled **ck**, as in qua**ck**, ne**ck**, qui**ck**, clo**ck**, and du**ck**.

The **/j/** sound after a short vowel is spelled **dge**, as in ba**dge**, ple**dge**, bri**dge**, do**dge**, and fu**dge**.

The **/z/** sound in **z**oo at the beginning of a root word is usually spelled **z** and **never** spelled **s**.

The **/sh/** sound at the beginning of a word or at the end of a syllable is usually spelled **sh**, as in **sh**eep and wi**sh**. At the beginning of any syllable after the first one, it is usually spelled **ti**, **si**, or **ci** (except for the ending **-ship**, as in friend**ship**), as in frac**ti**on, man**si**on, and spe**ci**al. When the syllable before it ends in **s**, as in mi**ssi**on, it is spelled **si**.

All, till, and full are usually spelled with one **l** when they are added to another syllable, as in a**l**most, unti**l**, and carefu**l**.

SPELLING RULES FOR VOWELS

The **/iy/** sound is **not** spelled **i** at the end of most words.

The **/ay/** sound is **not** spelled **a** at the end of root words.

The **/ee/** sound after **c** is spelled **ei**, as in rec**ei**ve.

The **/v/** sound at the end of a word is **never** spelled **v**. It is usually spelled **ve**, as in ha**ve**.

Jesus, Mary, Joseph, I love You. Save souls!

J.M.J.

PHONICS RULES FOR CONSONANTS

The letter **c** before **e**, **i**, or **y** makes the **/s/** sound, as in **c**ent, **c**ity, and **c**ycle. It makes the **/k/** sound before **a**, **o**, and **u**, as in **c**at, **c**old, and **c**up.

The letter **g** before **e**, **i**, or **y** sometimes makes the **/j/** sound, as in **g**em, **g**iant, and **g**ym. It usually makes the **/g/** sound before **a**, **o**, and **u**, as in **g**ame, **G**od, and **g**um.

The letters **si** between two vowels can make the **/zh/** sound, as in vi**si**on.

PHONICS RULES FOR VOWELS

The vowels **a**, **e**, **o**, and **u** at the end of a syllable usually make the long vowel sounds **/ay/**, **/ee/**, **/oh/**, and **/yoo/**, as in p**a**per, b**e**gin, **o**pen, and **u**nit.

The vowels **i** and **o** often make the long vowel sounds **/iy/** and **/oh/** when followed by two consonants, as in k**i**nd and g**o**ld.

The vowels **i** and **y** at the end of a syllable sometimes make the short vowel sound **/ih/**, as in fam**i**ly and bic**y**cle. However, they usually make the long vowel sound **/ee/** or **/iy/**, as in rad**i**o, wind**y**, m**y**, and f**i**nal.

The letters **or** after **w** often make the **/uhr/** sound, as in w**or**d.

The **silent final e** causes the preceding vowel to make its long sound, as in m**a**de, **e**ve, d**i**me, h**o**pe, and **u**se.

The **silent final e** causes the preceding **c** to make the **/s/** sound, as in chan**c**e.

The **silent final e** causes the preceding **g** to make the **/j/** sound, as in chan**g**e.

Rules for Dividing Words into Syllables

A one-syllable word cannot be divided.

Each syllable has only one vowel sound.

Divide between two vowels when they each make their own sound, as in qu**i·e**t.

Divide a compound word between the words.

Divide between two consonants, as in wi**n·d**ow. However, do not divide between two consonants that make one sound (a digraph), as in tel·e·**ph**one.

Divide before and after a vowel that makes its own sound, as in cav·**i**·ty.

Divide after the consonant when a short vowel sound is followed by a consonant and another vowel, as in H**eav·e**n.

Divide before the consonant when a long vowel sound is followed by a consonant and another vowel, as in p**a**·per.

When a word ending in -**le** is preceded by a consonant, divide the last syllable before the consonant, as in can·**dle** and fa·**ble**.

Divide between a base word and its prefix or suffix.

Rules for Capital Letters

The first word in a sentence begins with a capital letter.

A proper noun begins with a capital letter.

The important words in titles of proper nouns begin with capital letters.

Interjections are usually capitalized.

All names referring to the true God and the Bible are capitalized.

The pronoun **I** is always written with a capital letter.

In the salutation of a letter, the first word and the name of the person begin with capital letters. In the complimentary close, the first word is capitalized.

Rules for Forming Plurals

Plurals are formed by adding **s** or **es** to the singular noun.

Simply add **s** to most nouns.

Add **es** to nouns ending with **ss**, **x**, **z**, **ch**, or **sh**.

Change **y** to **i** before adding **es** when a noun ends with **y** preceded by a consonant. When a noun ends with **y** preceded by a vowel, simply add **s**.

Usually, when a noun ends with **f** or **fe**, simply add **s**. Sometimes change **f** or **fe** to **v** before adding **es**.

Add **es** to a noun ending with **o** preceded by a consonant (except for some musical terms, such as piano**s**). When a noun ends with **o** preceded by a vowel, simply add **s**.

The same rules for plurals of nouns apply to verbs in the present tense, third person, singular.

Rules for Adding Prefixes and Suffixes

Past-tense words ending in **-ed** make the **/d/** sound or **/t/** sound when the root ends with a letter other than **d** or **t**; otherwise, the ending -ed makes the **/ed/** sound.

Drop the **silent e** at the end of a word before adding a vowel suffix (prais**e**, prais**ing**).

Usually, keep the **silent e** at the end of a word before adding a consonant suffix.

Change **y** to **i** before adding a suffix that does not begin with **i** (cr**y**, cr**i**ed).

Double the final consonant of a short-vowel, one-syllable word before adding a vowel suffix (di**g**, di**gg**ing).

Double the final consonant of a two-syllable word ending with one consonant before adding a vowel suffix. However, when a suffix causes the stress to be moved to the first syllable of a word, do not double the final consonant (re·fer′, re·fe**rr**ed′, ref′·er·ence).

When the prefix **dis-**, **mis-**, or **un-** is added to a root word beginning with the same letter with which the prefix ends, double that letter (u**nn**ecessary, di**ss**olve, mi**ss**pell).

J.M.J.

Spelling 3 for Young Catholics

ANSWER KEY

Lesson 1:
Sight Words
A. Sort by Syllable
  1 syllable
    gone
    sew
    once
    eye
    else
    is
    been
    from
    one
    shall
    two
    as
    shoe
    laugh
  2 syllables
    only
    quiet

B. Complete Sentence
  1. as
  2. is
  3. one
  4. once
  5. two
  6. shoe
  7. from
  8. gone
  9. shall
  10. sew
  11. eye
  12. been
  13. else
  14. only
  15. quiet
  16. laugh

C. Alphabetical Order
  1. as
  2. been
  3. else
  4. eye
  5. from
  6. gone
  7. is

  8. laugh
  9. once
  10. one
  11. only
  12. quiet
  13. sew
  14. shall
  15. shoe
  16. two

D. Homophones
  1. been
  2. two
  3. eye
  4. one
  5. sew

Lesson 2:
Compound Words
A. Identify the Words
  pan   cake
  grape   vine
  can   not
  home   work
  rain   drop
  paint   brush
  grown   up
  side   walk
  back   pack
  farm   land
  sail   boat
  bath   tub
  farm   yard
  cow   boy
  play   ground
  mouse   trap

B. Complete Sentence
  1. bathtub
  2. cannot
  3. sailboat
  4. pancake
  5. cowboy
  6. playground
  7. grownup
  8. homework
  9. grapevine
  10. sidewalk
  11. backpack

  12. farmland
  13. farmyard
  14. raindrop
  15. paintbrush
  16. mousetrap

C. Alphabetical Order
  1. backpack
  2. bathtub
  3. cannot
  4. cowboy
  5. farmland
  6. farmyard
  7. grapevine
  8. grownup
  9. homework
  10. mousetrap
  11. paintbrush
  12. pancake
  13. playground
  14. raindrop
  15. sailboat
  16. sidewalk

D. Homophones
  1. grown
  2. sail

E. Rhyming Words
  1. mouse
  2. land
  3. yard
  4. boy
  5. ground
  6. bath

Lesson 3: /aa/
A. Sort by Syllable
  1 Syllable
    branch
  2 Syllables
    contact
    subtract
    after
    rabbit
    napkin
    answer
    sandwich
    Advent
    began

  catfish
  admit
  baptize
  3 Syllables
    cavity
    animal
    Catholic

B. Complete Sentence
  1. branch
  2. subtract
  3. after
  4. rabbit
  5. sandwich
  6. Advent
  7. napkin
  8. answer
  9. admit
  10. contact
  11. began
  12. catfish
  13. baptize
  14. cavity
  15. animal
  16. Catholic

C. Alphabetical Order
  1. admit
  2. Advent
  3. after
  4. animal
  5. answer
  6. baptize
  7. began
  8. branch
  9. catfish
  10. Catholic
  11. cavity
  12. contact
  13. napkin
  14. rabbit
  15. sandwich
  16. subtract

D. Syllables
  1. subtract
  2. napkin
  3. sandwich
  4. Advent
  5. animal, answer

Jesus, Mary, Joseph, I love You. Save souls!

Lesson 4: /eh/
A. Sort by Spelling
e
- letter
- confess
- second
- lesson
- never
- telephone

ea
- bread
- read
- head
- spread
- dead
- Heaven
- breakfast

Sight words
- again
- any
- many

B. Complete Sentence
1. bread
2. breakfast
3. Heaven
4. letter
5. lesson
6. never
7. read
8. confess
9. dead
10. head
11. second
12. any
13. many
14. again
15. spread
16. telephone

C. Alphabetical Order
1. again
2. any
3. bread
4. breakfast
5. confess
6. dead
7. head
8. Heaven
9. lesson
10. letter
11. many
12. never
13. read
14. second
15. spread
16. telephone

D. Homophones
1. read
2. lesson

E. Rhyming Words
1. never
2. Heaven
3. again

F. Syllables
1. breakfast
2. telephone
3. letter

Lesson 5: /ih/
A. Sort by Spelling
i
- give
- picture
- pitcher
- minute
- hidden
- different
- Indian
- river
- begin
- children
- live
- America

y
- hymnal
- myth
- gypsy

ui
- build

B. Complete Sentence
1. myth
2. gypsy
3. hymnal
4. build
5. picture
6. pitcher
7. minute
8. Begin
9. children
10. hidden
11. different
12. Indian
13. river
14. give
15. live
16. America

C. Alphabetical Order
1. America
2. begin
3. build
4. children
5. different
6. give
7. gypsy
8. hidden
9. hymnal
10. Indian
11. live
12. minute
13. myth
14. picture
15. pitcher
16. river

D. Rhyming Words
1. myth
2. build
3. river
4. live

E. Syllables
1. hidden
2. Indian
3. begin

Lesson 6: /ah/
A. Sort by Spelling
o
- upon
- beyond
- homily
- dollar
- honor
- lot
- boxes
- doctor
- apostle

a
- father
- watch
- Amen
- wand
- hurrah
- wander
- koala

B. Complete Sentence
1. boxes
2. beyond
3. homily
4. dollar
5. upon
6. Amen
7. Hurrah
8. Father
9. koala
10. Honor
11. doctor
12. lot
13. wand
14. wander
15. Watch
16. Apostle

C. Alphabetical Order
1. Amen
2. apostle
3. beyond
4. boxes
5. doctor
6. dollar
7. father
8. homily
9. honor
10. hurrah
11. koala
12. lot
13. upon
14. wand
15. wander
16. watch

D. Rhyming Words
1. watch
2. wand, beyond
3. dollar
4. lot
5. boxes
6. apostle

E. Syllables
1. Amen
2. upon

Lesson 7: /aw/
A. Sort by Spelling
a
- always
- water
- also
- mall

o
- often
- soggy

aw
- saw
- yawn
- awful
- awe

au
- pause
- sauce
- because

ough
- thought

Answer Key • Spelling 3 for Young Catholics   J.M.J.

augh
  taught
  daughter

B. Complete Sentence
1. awe
2. saw
3. awful
4. often
5. yawn
6. always
7. soggy
8. because
9. Pause
10. sauce
11. water
12. mall
13. also
14. taught
15. thought
16. daughter

C. Alphabetical Order
1. also
2. always
3. awe
4. awful
5. because
6. daughter
7. mall
8. often
9. pause
10. sauce
11. saw
12. soggy
13. taught
14. thought
15. water
16. yawn

D. Homophones
1. taught
2. pause
3. mall

E. Rhyming Words
1. soggy
2. thought, taught
3. yawn
4. mall

Lesson 8: /uh/
A. Sort by Spelling
u
  butter
  begun
  bunch
  number

sunny
under
until

ou
  country
  enough

o
  above
  love
  son
  sometimes
  other
  mother
  another

B. Complete Sentence
1. sunny
2. butter
3. bunch
4. Son
5. country
6. number
7. other
8. Mother
9. another
10. begun
11. Love
12. under
13. until
14. above
15. Sometimes
16. enough

C. Alphabetical Order
1. above
2. another
3. begun
4. bunch
5. butter
6. country
7. enough
8. love
9. mother
10. number
11. other
12. sometimes
13. son
14. sunny
15. under
16. until

D. Homophone
  son

E. Rhyming Words
1. love, above
2. mother, other, another

3. enough
4. son

F. Syllables
1. sometimes
2. sunny
3. butter

Lesson 9: Review
Lesson 1 Words
gone
sew
once
eye
else
is
on·ly
been
from
one
qui·et
shall
two
as
shoe
laugh

Lesson 2 Words
pan·cake
grape·vine
can·not
home·work
rain·drop
paint·brush
grown·up
side·walk
back·pack
farm·land
sail·boat
bath·tub
farm·yard
cow·boy
play·ground
mouse·trap

Lesson 3 Words
cav·i·ty
con·tact
sub·tract
af·ter
rab·bit
nap·kin
an·swer
sand·wich
Ad·vent
be·gan
cat·fish
ad·mit

an·i·mal
branch
bap·tize
Cath·o·lic

Lesson 4 Words
let·ter
bread
a·gain
read
con·fess
an·y
head
man·y
spread
dead
sec·ond
Heav·en
les·son
break·fast
nev·er
tel·e·phone

Lesson 5 Words
give
pic·ture
pitch·er
min·ute
hid·den
hym·nal
dif·fer·ent
myth
In·di·an
build
riv·er
gyp·sy moth
be·gin
chil·dren
live
A·mer·i·ca

Lesson 6 Words
fa·ther
up·on
watch
A·men
wand
be·yond
hom·i·ly
dol·lar
hur·rah
hon·or
lot
wan·der
ko·a·la
box·es
doc·tor
a·pos·tle

Lesson 7 Words
saw
thought
of·ten
yawn
taught
al·ways
sog·gy
pause
aw·ful
awe
sauce
wa·ter
al·so
be·cause
mall
daugh·ter

Lesson 8 Words
but·ter
coun·try
a·bove
be·gun
love
bunch
son
some·times
num·ber
oth·er
moth·er
sun·ny
an·oth·er
un·der
un·til
e·nough

Lesson 10: /k/, /s/
A. Identify Spellings
/k/
c
  cir**c**us
  cricket
  a**cc**ept
  cate**c**hism
ch
  Christmas
  cate**ch**ism
ck
  cri**ck**et
k
  kitchen
  kept
qu
  uni**qu**e
  mos**qu**ito

/s/
s
  rece**ss**
  circu**s**
  Christma**s**
  mo**s**quito
c
  city
  pen**c**il
  re**c**ess
  circus
  ac**c**ept
  ex**c**ept
  balan**c**e
sc
  scent
  scene

B. Complete Sentence
1. cricket
2. Christmas
3. kitchen
4. catechism
5. unique
6. accept
7. except
8. kept
9. city
10. scent
11. circus
12. scene
13. pencil
14. recess
15. balance
16. mosquito

C. Alphabetical Order
1. accept
2. balance
3. catechism
4. Christmas
5. circus
6. city
7. cricket
8. except
9. kept
10. kitchen
11. mosquito
12. pencil
13. recess
14. scene
15. scent
16. unique

D. Homophones
1. scent
2. scene

E. Rhyming Words
1. kept, accept, except
2. city

F. Syllables
1. pencil
2. catechism
3. Christmas

Lesson 11: /j/, /z/
A. Sort by Spelling
/j/
j
  Jim
dge
  fudge
  badge
g
  gentle
  gym
  change
  tragic

/z/
z
  sneeze
  zero
s
  these
  close
  please
  cheese
  scissors
  those
x
  xylophone

B. Complete Sentence
1. Jim
2. gym
3. badge
4. fudge
5. please
6. tragic
7. change
8. zero
9. Gentle
10. sneeze
11. cheese
12. close
13. scissors
14. these
15. those
16. xylophone

C. Alphabetical Order
1. badge
2. change
3. cheese
4. close
5. fudge
6. gentle
7. gym
8. Jim
9. please
10. scissors
11. sneeze
12. these
13. those
14. tragic
15. xylophone
16. zero

D. Homophones
1. gym
2. close

E. Rhyming Words
1. fudge
2. close, those
3. sneeze, these, please, cheese
4. zero
5. change

Lesson 12: Silent Consonants
A. Sort by Silent Letter
b
  debts
  lamb
g
  gnat
h
  rhyme
  hour
  ghost
k
  knot
  knock
  knife
  kneel
l
  half
  yolk
n
  hymn
p
  Psalms
w
  whole
  wrote

B. Complete Sentence
1. Ghost
2. kneel

Answer Key • Spelling 3 for Young Catholics   J.M.J.

3. knock
4. gnat
5. yolk
6. wrote
7. whole
8. debts
9. lamb
10. knot
11. half
12. hymn
13. rhyme
14. hour
15. knife
16. Psalms

C. Alphabetical Order
1. debts
2. ghost
3. gnat
4. half
5. hour
6. hymn
7. kneel
8. knife
9. knock
10. knot
11. lamb
12. Psalms
13. rhyme
14. whole
15. wrote
16. yolk

D. Homophones
1. yolk
2. wrote
3. hymn
4. whole
5. rhyme
6. knot

E. Rhyming Words
1. half
2. lamb
3. ghost

Lesson 13: /ng/
A. Sort by Spelling
ng
   ring
   king
   strong
   long
   string
   spring
   wrong
   thing
   wing
   bring
   song
   young
n
   bank
   sink
   think
   thank

B. Complete Sentence
1. think
2. song
3. long
4. sink
5. King
6. strong
7. wrong
8. bank
9. bring
10. spring
11. string
12. Thank
13. wing
14. young
15. thing
16. ring

C. Alphabetical Order
1. bank
2. bring
3. king
4. long
5. ring
6. sink
7. song
8. spring
9. string
10. strong
11. thank
12. thing
13. think
14. wing
15. wrong
16. young

D. Homophone
ring

E. Rhyming Words
1. young
2. sink, think
3. bank, thank
4. strong, long, wrong, song
5. ring, king, string, spring, thing, wing, bring

Lesson 14: /ay/
A. Sort by Spelling
a
   pavement
   paper
   waste
   favorite
ay
   away
   mayor
   gray
   crayon
ai
   mail
eigh
   weigh
   eight
ey
   they
   obey
ea
   break
   great
ei
   vein

B. Complete Sentence
1. vein
2. waste
3. gray
4. mail
5. eight
6. They
7. break
8. paper
9. great
10. weigh
11. mayor
12. pavement
13. away
14. crayon
15. obey
16. favorite

C. Alphabetical Order
1. away
2. break
3. crayon
4. eight
5. favorite
6. gray
7. great
8. mail
9. mayor
10. obey
11. paper
12. pavement
13. they
14. vein
15. waste
16. weigh

D. Homophones
1. eight
2. waste
3. break
4. weigh
5. vein
6. great
7. mail

Lesson 15: /ee/
A. Sort by Spelling
e
   even
ea
   really
   Easter
ee
   between
ey
   key
y
   study
   carry
   every
   daily
   lonely
   very
   family
i
   radio
ie
   movie
   relief
   priest

B. Complete Sentence
1. Easter
2. Study
3. even
4. between
5. very
6. radio
7. movie
8. carry
9. every
10. family
11. daily
12. really
13. lonely
14. relief
15. priest

16. key

C. Alphabetical Order
1. between
2. carry
3. daily
4. Easter
5. even
6. every
7. family
8. key
9. lonely
10. movie
11. priest
12. radio
13. really
14. relief
15. study
16. very

D. Rhyming Words
1. priest
2. even
3. relief
4. very, carry
5. lonely

E. Syllables
1. really
2. between

Lesson 16: /iy/
A. Sort by Spelling
i
  private
  write
  while
  tiger
  idea
  like
ie
  die
igh
  might
  light
  high
  right
  sight
  night
i and y
  identify
ui
  guide
Sight word
  buy

B. Complete Sentence
1. tiger
2. private
3. high
4. light
5. might
6. die
7. guide
8. like
9. right
10. write
11. buy
12. night
13. while
14. sight
15. idea
16. Identify

C. Alphabetical Order
1. buy
2. die
3. guide
4. high
5. idea
6. identify
7. light
8. like
9. might
10. night
11. private
12. right
13. sight
14. tiger
15. while
16. write

D. Homophones
1. buy
2. high
3. die
4. right, write
5. sight
6. night
7. might

Lesson 17: /oh/
A. Sort by Spelling
o
  over
  almost
  open
  notice
  rose
  holy
ow
  window
  follow
  below
  knows
  yellow
  own
  owe
ough
  dough
  though
oa
  groan

B. Complete Sentence
1. almost
2. knows
3. dough
4. below
5. window
6. yellow
7. over
8. groan
9. holy
10. rose
11. Follow
12. own
13. notice
14. open
15. owe
16. though

C. Alphabetical Order
1. almost
2. below
3. dough
4. follow
5. groan
6. holy
7. knows
8. notice
9. open
10. over
11. owe
12. own
13. rose
14. though
15. window
16. yellow

D. Homophones
1. holy
2. groan
3. dough
4. rose
5. owe
6. knows

E. Syllable
  almost

Lesson 18: Review
Lesson 10 Words
scent
kitch·en
kept
cit·y
pen·cil
re·cess
crick·et
cir·cus
u·nique
bal·ance
ac·cept
scene
Christ·mas
cat·e·chism
ex·cept
mos·qui·to

Lesson 11 Words
gen·tle
sneeze
ze·ro
these
gym
fudge
Jim
close
change
badge
please
cheese
scis·sors
trag·ic
those
xy·lo·phone

Lesson 12 Words
gnat
debts
knot
half
lamb
whole
hymn
yolk
wrote
knock
rhyme
hour
knife
ghost
kneel
Psalms

Lesson 13 Words
ring
king
strong
long
bank
string

Answer Key • Spelling 3 for Young Catholics   J.M.J.

spring
sink
think
thank
wrong
thing
wing
bring
song
young

Lesson 14 Words
break
they
vein
mail
pave·ment
a·way
weigh
may·or
pa·per
great
gray
cray·on
eight
waste
o·bey
fa·vor·ite

Lesson 15 Words
real·ly
e·ven
be·tween
stud·y
car·ry
eve·ry
mov·ie
key
dai·ly
ra·di·o
Eas·ter
lone·ly
re·lief
ver·y
fam·i·ly
priest

Lesson 16 Words
might
light
high
pri·vate
write
while
right
ti·ger
buy
sight

i·de·a
guide
like
die
night
i·den·ti·fy

Lesson 17 Words
win·dow
dough
o·ver
groan
fol·low
be·low
al·most
o·pen
knows
no·tice
yel·low
own
rose
ho·ly
owe
though

Lesson 19: /yoo/
A. Sort by Spelling
u
  usual
  unit
  unite
  cubic
  use
  confuse
  menu
  refuse
  humor
  music
  future
  human
  uniform
ue
  rescue
ew
  nephew
Sight word
  beauty

B. Complete Sentence
1. music
2. nephew
3. future
4. use
5. confuse
6. refuse
7. humor
8. human
9. menu

10. uniform
11. rescue
12. usual
13. beauty
14. unite
15. unit
16. cubic

C. Alphabetical Order
1. beauty
2. confuse
3. cubic
4. future
5. human
6. humor
7. menu
8. music
9. nephew
10. refuse
11. rescue
12. uniform
13. unit
14. unite
15. use
16. usual

D. Rhyming Words
1. humor
2. future
3. nephew, menu, rescue
4. beauty

E. Syllables
1. confuse, refuse
2. uniform
3. human

Lesson 20: /ooh/
A. Sort by Spelling
oo
  school
  zoo
  cocoon
o
  into
  move
ew
  screw
  new
  stew
  knew
ue
  statue
ui
  fruit
ough
  through

ou
  group
eu
  neutral
u
  rule
  truth

B. Complete Sentence
1. zoo
2. move
3. screw
4. statue
5. group
6. into
7. rule
8. neutral
9. cocoon
10. knew
11. School
12. new
13. stew
14. truth
15. fruit
16. through

C. Alphabetical Order
1. cocoon
2. fruit
3. group
4. into
5. knew
6. move
7. neutral
8. new
9. rule
10. school
11. screw
12. statue
13. stew
14. through
15. truth
16. zoo

D. Homophones
1. knew, new
2. through

E. Rhyming Words
1. group
2. rule, school
3. fruit
4. move
5. truth

Lesson 21: /uu/
A. Sort by Spelling
oo
  shook

hood
hook
wooden
hooray
cookie
wool
woodpecker
u
  sugar
  pulpit
  butcher
  bully
  bushel
ou
  would
  could
  should

B. Complete Sentence
1. cookie
2. shook
3. sugar
4. wooden
5. wool
6. hood
7. hook
8. Hooray
9. bushel
10. butcher
11. bully
12. pulpit
13. should
14. could
15. Would
16. woodpecker

C. Alphabetical Order
1. bully
2. bushel
3. butcher
4. cookie
5. could
6. hood
7. hook
8. hooray
9. pulpit
10. shook
11. should
12. sugar
13. wooden
14. woodpecker
15. wool
16. would

D. Homophone
  would

E. Rhyming Words
1. would, hood,

    could, should
2. shook, hook

F. Syllables
1. cookie
2. bushel
3. wooden, woodpecker
4. hooray
5. pulpit

Lesson 22: /uhr/
A. Sort by Spelling
ur
  urn
  furnace
  hurry
er
  berth
  person
ir
  squirm
  birthday
or
  worldwide
  worry
  workbook
ear
  earn
  learn
  early
  earth
  earthquake
Sight word
  journey

B. Complete Sentence
1. earn
2. hurry
3. Earth
4. learn
5. person
6. earthquake
7. Birthday
8. furnace
9. squirm
10. early
11. workbook
12. worldwide
13. worry
14. journey
15. urn
16. berth

C. Alphabetical Order
1. berth
2. birthday
3. early
4. earn
5. earth
6. earthquake
7. furnace
8. hurry
9. journey
10. learn
11. person
12. squirm
13. urn
14. workbook
15. worldwide
16. worry

D. Homophones
1. earn
2. berth

E. Syllables
1. earth, earthquake
2. worldwide
3. furnace
4. birthday
5. workbook

Lesson 23: /ahr/
A. Sort by Spelling
ar
  bargain
  part
  scar
  guard
  card
  arm
  garden
  hard
  harvest
  art
  stars
  charge
  carpet
  bark
  faraway
ear
  heart

B. Complete Sentence
1. carpet
2. scar
3. arm
4. art
5. card
6. bark
7. part
8. Guard
9. heart
10. garden
11. hard
12. harvest
13. bargain
14. stars
15. charge
16. faraway

C. Alphabetical Order
1. arm
2. art
3. bargain
4. bark
5. card
6. carpet
7. charge
8. faraway
9. garden
10. guard
11. hard
12. harvest
13. heart
14. part
15. scar
16. stars

D. Rhyming Words
1. part, heart, art
2. guard, card, hard
3. charge
4. bark
5. garden
6. scar

E. Syllable
  carpet

Lesson 24: /ayr/
A. Sort by Spelling
air
  pair
  stair
  air
  chair
  haircut
are
  scared
  square
  care
  stare
  share
ear
  bear
  wear
  tear
  pear
eir
  their
Sight word
  prayer

Answer Key • Spelling 3 for Young Catholics   J.M.J.

B. Complete Sentence
1. care
2. tear
3. air
4. chair
5. Wear
6. stair
7. stare
8. bear
9. pair
10. pear
11. scared
12. share
13. square
14. prayer
15. their
16. haircut

C. Alphabetical Order
1. air
2. bear
3. care
4. chair
5. haircut
6. pair
7. pear
8. prayer
9. scared
10. share
11. square
12. stair
13. stare
14. tear
15. their
16. wear

D. Homophones
1. bear
2. wear
3. their
4. pair, pear
5. stare

E. Rhyming Word
scared

F. Syllable
haircut

Lesson 25: /eer/
A. Sort by Spelling
ear
  tear
  near
  clear
  year
  hear
  fear
  earring

dear
ere
  here
eer
  peer
  deer
eir
  weird
ier
  pier
  fierce
  pierce
  tier

B. Complete Sentence
1. fierce
2. year
3. dear
4. deer
5. clear
6. Peer
7. pier
8. tear
9. fear
10. near
11. hear
12. here
13. earring
14. weird
15. tier
16. pierce

C. Alphabetical Order
1. clear
2. dear
3. deer
4. earring
5. fear
6. fierce
7. hear
8. here
9. near
10. peer
11. pier
12. pierce
13. tear
14. tier
15. weird
16. year

D. Homophones
1. peer
2. dear
3. tear
4. here

E. Rhyming Words
1. weird
2. fierce

F. Letters
tear, near, clear, year, hear, fear, dear

Lesson 26: /ohr/
A. Sort by Spelling
oar
  oar
or
  or
  short
  Lord
  corn
  story
  form
  for
  record
ore
  more
  before
  sore
  ore
  store
our
  four
  pour

B. Complete Sentence
1. or
2. oar
3. ore
4. four
5. store
6. short
7. Pour
8. sore
9. form
10. before
11. story
12. for
13. more
14. Lord
15. corn
16. record

C. Alphabetical Order
1. before
2. corn
3. for
4. form
5. four
6. Lord
7. more
8. oar
9. or
10. ore

11. pour
12. record
13. short
14. sore
15. store
16. story

D. Homophones
1. oar, ore
2. four, for
3. sore
4. pour

E. Rhyming Words
1. Lord, record
2. short
3. corn
4. form

Lesson 27: Review
Lesson 19 Words
beau·ty
u·su·al
u·nit
u·nite
cu·bic
use
con·fuse
neph·ew
men·u
re·fuse (verb)
or ref·use (noun)
hu·mor
mu·sic
res·cue
fu·ture
hu·man
u·ni·form

Lesson 20 Words
screw
group
in·to
rule
new
fruit
stew
stat·ue
move
knew
school
zoo
neu·tral
truth
co·coon
through

Lesson 21 Words
sug·ar

pul·pit
would
shook
hood
hook
butch·er
could
wood·en
bul·ly
hoo·ray
should
cook·ie
bush·el
wool
wood·peck·er

Lesson 22 Words
urn
berth
per·son
earn
learn
world·wide
wor·ry
fur·nace
squirm
ear·ly
work·book
hur·ry
earth
birth·day
earth·quake
jour·ney

Lesson 23 Words
bar·gain
part
scar
guard
card
arm
heart
gar·den
hard
har·vest
art
stars
charge
car·pet
bark
far·a·way

Lesson 24 Words
bear
wear
scared
pair
square

stair
their
care
tear
stare
pear
air
chair
hair·cut
share
prayer

Lesson 25 Words
peer
pier
fierce
deer
here
tear
near
clear
pierce
year
hear
fear
ear·ring
tier
dear
weird

Lesson 26 Words
four
pour
more
be·fore
or
short
sore
Lord
corn
ore
sto·ry
store
form
oar
for
re·cord (verb)
or rec·ord (noun)

Lesson 28: /ou/
A. Sort by Spelling
ou
  mouse
  our
  without
  mountain
  sound

sour
found
around
about
cloud
outside
thousand
ow
  flower
  crowd
  down
ough
  drought

B. Complete Sentence
1. outside
2. about
3. crowd
4. sound
5. around
6. cloud
7. mouse
8. our
9. down
10. found
11. sour
12. thousand
13. mountain
14. flower
15. without
16. drought

C. Alphabetical Order
1. about
2. around
3. cloud
4. crowd
5. down
6. drought
7. flower
8. found
9. mountain
10. mouse
11. our
12. outside
13. sound
14. sour
15. thousand
16. without

D. Homophones
1. our
2. flower

E. Rhyming Words
1. mouse
2. crowd, cloud
3. about, without,

drought

F. Syllable
outside, without

Lesson 29: /oi/
A. Sort by Spelling
oi
  moisture
  noise
  ointment
  spoil
  appoint
  poison
  avoid
  rejoice
  foil
  noisy
  embroider
oy
  soybean
  voyage
  oyster
  royal
  annoy

B. Complete Sentence
1. spoil
2. noisy
3. rejoice
4. avoid
5. appoint
6. royal
7. oyster
8. ointment
9. moisture
10. noise
11. annoy
12. voyage
13. soybean
14. foil
15. embroider
16. poison

C. Alphabetical Order
1. annoy
2. appoint
3. avoid
4. embroider
5. foil
6. moisture
7. noise
8. noisy
9. ointment
10. oyster
11. poison
12. rejoice
13. royal

Answer Key • Spelling 3 for Young Catholics   J.M.J.

14. soybean
15. spoil
16. voyage

D. Rhyming Words
1. spoil, foil, royal
2. noise
3. annoy
4. rejoice
5. oyster
6. appoint
7. avoid
8. ointment

Lesson 30: /sh/
A. Sort by Spelling
ti
  fraction
  position
  direction
  nation
  solution
  equation
  station
  caution
  section
  option
  action
si
  mission
  mansion
  passion
ci
  special
ch
  machine

B. Complete Sentence
1. action
2. caution
3. Station
4. option
5. section
6. mansion
7. Passion
8. mission
9. nation
10. fraction
11. equation
12. direction
13. position
14. solution
15. machine
16. special

C. Alphabetical Order
1. action
2. caution
3. direction
4. equation
5. fraction
6. machine
7. mansion
8. mission
9. nation
10. option
11. passion
12. position
13. section
14. solution
15. special
16. station

D. Root Words
1. passion
2. direction
3. mansion
4. mission
5. option

Lesson 31: -le
A. Sort by Syllable
2 syllables
  Bible
  ankle
  circle
  fable
  paddle
  whistle
  bottle
  middle
  little
  candle
  bubble
  table
  people
3 syllables
  bicycle
  example
  article

B. Complete Sentence
1. candle
2. Bible
3. middle
4. ankle
5. bubble
6. table
7. little
8. example
9. circle
10. bicycle
11. fable
12. people
13. whistle
14. bottle
15. paddle
16. article

C. Alphabetical Order
1. ankle
2. article
3. Bible
4. bicycle
5. bottle
6. bubble
7. candle
8. circle
9. example
10. fable
11. little
12. middle
13. paddle
14. people
15. table
16. whistle

D. Rhyming Words
1. table, fable
2. bubble
3. candle
4. middle
5. people
6. article
7. little
8. example
9. bicycle
10. paddle

Lesson 32: -s, -es
A. Form Plurals
1. angels
2. sacraments
3. prayers
4. sisters
5. radios
6. brothers
7. beliefs
8. wishes
9. watches
10. cherries
11. berries
12. hobbies
13. wolves
14. knives
15. heroes
16. gives

B. Complete Sentence
1. sisters
2. prayers
3. angels
4. cherries
5. berries
6. hobbies
7. radios
8. heroes
9. brothers
10. gives
11. knives
12. wolves
13. wishes
14. watches
15. sacraments
16. beliefs

C. Alphabetical Order
1. angels
2. beliefs
3. berries
4. brothers
5. cherries
6. gives
7. heroes
8. hobbies
9. knives
10. prayers
11. radios
12. sacraments
13. sisters
14. watches
15. wishes
16. wolves

D. Write Plurals
1. radios
2. berries
3. beliefs
4. wolves
5. prayers
6. knives
7. heroes
8. wishes

Lesson 33: -ing
A. Add the Ending -ing
1. praising
2. giving
3. digging
4. forgetting
5. praying
6. staying
7. crying
8. preaching
9. jumping
10. going
11. trusting
12. fasting
13. spelling
14. blessing

15. walking
16. floating

B. Complete Sentence
1. floating
2. going
3. giving
4. praying
5. spelling
6. staying
7. crying
8. fasting
9. trusting
10. preaching
11. praising
12. walking
13. digging
14. jumping
15. blessing
16. forgetting

C. Alphabetical Order
1. blessing
2. crying
3. digging
4. fasting
5. floating
6. forgetting
7. giving
8. going
9. jumping
10. praising
11. praying
12. preaching
13. spelling
14. staying
15. trusting
16. walking

D. Syllables
1. staying
2. preaching
3. crying
4. walking
5. blessing
6. spelling
7. praying

Lesson 34: -ed
A. Add Ending -ed
1. graded
2. framed
3. lived
4. praised
5. planned
6. cried
7. tried
8. roasted
9. kissed
10. wanted
11. laughed
12. started
13. missed
14. stayed
15. looked
16. called

B. Complete Sentence
1. framed
2. roasted
3. started
4. praised
5. wanted
6. stayed
7. cried
8. called
9. lived
10. looked
11. tried
12. graded
13. kissed
14. missed
15. laughed
16. planned

C. Alphabetical Order
1. called
2. cried
3. framed
4. graded
5. kissed
6. laughed
7. lived
8. looked
9. missed
10. planned
11. praised
12. roasted
13. started
14. stayed
15. tried
16. wanted

D. Sort by Sound
1. framed, tried, planned, praised, cried, stayed, lived, called
2. missed, laughed, looked, kissed
3. roasted, graded, started, wanted

Lesson 35: -ly, -ful
A. Sort by Suffix
-ful
  wonderful
  thankful
  graceful
  careful
-fully
  beautifully
  faithfully
-ly
  finally
  annually
  hourly
  fatherly
  friendly
  weekly
  monthly
  motherly
  lively
  usually

B. Complete Sentence
1. motherly
2. Fatherly
3. friendly
4. lively
5. finally
6. hourly
7. weekly
8. monthly
9. annually
10. thankful
11. wonderful
12. graceful
13. faithfully
14. beautifully
15. careful
16. usually

C. Alphabetical Order
1. annually
2. beautifully
3. careful
4. faithfully
5. fatherly
6. finally
7. friendly
8. graceful
9. hourly
10. lively
11. monthly
12. motherly
13. thankful
14. usually
15. weekly
16. wonderful

D. Syllables
1. wonderful
2. annually
3. beautifully
4. fatherly
5. motherly

Lesson 36: Review
Lesson 28 Words
mouse
flow·er
our
with·out
moun·tain
sound
sour
found
a·round
a·bout
crowd
down
cloud
out·side
thou·sand
drought

Lesson 29 Words
soy·bean
mois·ture
noise
oint·ment
spoil
voy·age
ap·point
oys·ter
poi·son
a·void
re·joice
roy·al
an·noy
foil
nois·y
em·broi·der

Lesson 30 Words
mis·sion
frac·tion
po·si·tion
di·rec·tion
man·sion
pas·sion
na·tion
so·lu·tion
e·qua·tion
sta·tion
cau·tion
sec·tion

Answer Key • Spelling 3 for Young Catholics J.M.J.

op·tion
ac·tion
ma·chine
spe·cial

Lesson 31 Words
Bi·ble
an·kle
cir·cle
fa·ble
pad·dle
whis·tle
bot·tle
mid·dle
lit·tle
can·dle
bub·ble
bi·cy·cle
ta·ble
ex·am·ple
peo·ple
ar·ti·cle

Lesson 32 Words
cher·ries
be·liefs
sis·ters
wish·es
he·roes
ber·ries
watch·es
broth·ers
gives
prayers
hob·bies
an·gels
knives
wolves
ra·di·os
sac·ra·ments

Lesson 33 Words
stay·ing
preach·ing
prais·ing
cry·ing
fast·ing
go·ing
walk·ing
bless·ing
giv·ing
float·ing
spell·ing
dig·ging
pray·ing
trust·ing
jump·ing
for·get·ting

Lesson 34 Words
roast·ed
grad·ed
framed
planned
cried
want·ed
lived
start·ed
tried
missed
praised
stayed
called
looked
kissed
laughed

Lesson 35 Words
fi·nal·ly
won·der·ful
an·nu·al·ly
thank·ful
hour·ly
grace·ful
care·ful
beau·ti·ful·ly
fa·ther·ly
friend·ly
week·ly
month·ly
moth·er·ly
faith·ful·ly
live·ly
u·su·al·ly

List of Artists

Page	Title	Artist
iv	Holy Family with St. John	Gentileschi
vi	Holy Family with St. John	Murillo
1	Education of the Virgin	Jouvenet
6	St. Philip Neri	Tiepolo
7	St. Luke Painting Mary and Jesus	Vasari
16	The Baptism of Christ	Murillo
17	Return of the Prodigal Son	Murillo
26	Let the Children Come to Me	Bloch
27	Christ Gives the Keys to Peter	Champaigne
36	Adoration of the Magi	Lippi
37	The Annunciation	Murillo
48	The Nativity	Rubens
49	Madonna and Child	Rubens
58	David Plays the Harp Before Saul	de Bray
59	Mystical Marriage of St. Catherine	Rubens
68	Christ Teaching at the Temple	Bloch
69	Resurrection	Titan
78	Christ Healing the Blind	Champaigne
79	The Crucifixion	Perugino
90	Our Lady of Seville	Murillo
91	Agony in the Garden	Hofmann
100	Peter Preaching	Kulmbach
101	The Creation	Doré
110	Behold the Man	Ciseri
111	St. James the Greater	Batoni
120	The Lance	Tissot
121	Jonas Leaving the Whale	Bruegel
132	The Loaves and the Fishes	Unknown Dutch artist
133	Resurrection	van Dyck
142	Carrying the Cross	Bassano
143	Jesus Preaching on a Boat	Tissot
152	The Good Shepherd	Champaigne
153	St. Paul in Athens	Raphael
162	The Garden of Eden	Wenzel
163	Madonna and Child	Raphael

Jesus, Mary, Joseph, I love You. Save souls!

Selected Bibliography

While the editors of this workbook utilized a host of resources in order to compile the most comprehensive word lists possible for this text, the following are a few of the sources that proved particularly helpful.

Editors of the American Heritage® Dictionaries. *American Heritage® Children's Dictionary, The.* Boston: Houghton-Mifflin, 1998.

Foltzer, Monica, M.Ed. *Professor Phonics Gives Sound Advice.* Cincinnati: St. Ursula Academy, 1995.

Fry, Edward Bernard, Ph.D., Jacqueline E. Kress, Ed.D., and Dona Lee Fountoukidis, Ed.D. *The Reading Teacher's Book of Lists, Third Edition.* Paramus, NJ: Prentice Hall, 1993.

http://www.dictionary.com

Maples, Mary Lou, Ed.D. et al. *Spectrum Phonics: Grade 3.* McGraw-Hill Learning Materials, 1998.

Pescosolido, John R., Ph.D. et al. *Spelling Level 3.* Steck-Vaughn Company, 1996.

Roser, Dr. Nancy L. and Dr. Jean Wallace Gillet. *SRA Spelling Cardinal Supplement. Level 3.* Columbus: SRA/McGraw-Hill, 1999.

Rudginsky, Laura Toby and Elizabeth C. Haskell. *How to Spell: Workbook 3.* Cambridge, MA: Educators Publishing Service, Inc., 1998.

Spelling Activity Workbook. Level 3. New York: McGraw-Hill School Division, 1998.

# Practice

J.M.J.

1.
2.
3.
4.
5.
6.
7.
8.
9.
10.
11.
12.
13.
14.
15.
16.

1.
2.
3.
4.
5.
6.
7.
8.
9.
10.
11.
12.
13.
14.
15.
16.

Jesus, Mary, Joseph, I love You. Save souls!

Practice

J.M.J.

1.	1.
2.	2.
3.	3.
4.	4.
5.	5.
6.	6.
7.	7.
8.	8.
9.	9.
10.	10.
11.	11.
12.	12.
13.	13.
14.	14.
15.	15.
16.	16.

Jesus, Mary, Joseph, I love You. Save souls!

Practice

J.M.J.

1.
2.
3.
4.
5.
6.
7.
8.
9.
10.
11.
12.
13.
14.
15.
16.

1.
2.
3.
4.
5.
6.
7.
8.
9.
10.
11.
12.
13.
14.
15.
16.

Jesus, Mary, Joseph, I love You. Save souls!

J.M.J.

Practice

1.	1.
2.	2.
3.	3.
4.	4.
5.	5.
6.	6.
7.	7.
8.	8.
9.	9.
10.	10.
11.	11.
12.	12.
13.	13.
14.	14.
15.	15.
16.	16.

Jesus, Mary, Joseph, I love You. Save souls!

Practice

J.M.J.

1.	1.
2.	2.
3.	3.
4.	4.
5.	5.
6.	6.
7.	7.
8.	8.
9.	9.
10.	10.
11.	11.
12.	12.
13.	13.
14.	14.
15.	15.
16.	16.

Jesus, Mary, Joseph, I love You. Save souls!

Like our books?

You might like our program, too. Seton Home Study School offers a full curriculum program for Pre-Kindergarten through Twelfth Grade. We include daily lesson plans, answer keys, quarterly tests, and much more. Our staff of teachers and counselors is available to answer questions and offer help. We keep student records and send out diplomas that are backed by our accreditation with the Southern Association of Colleges and Schools and the AdvancEd Accreditation Commission.

For more information about Seton Home Study School, please contact our admissions office.

Seton Home Study School
1350 Progress Drive
Front Royal, VA 22630

Phone: 540-636-9990 • Fax: 540-636-1602
Internet: www.setonhome.org • E-mail: info@setonhome.org